76 Ways to Protect Your Child from Crime

Other books by J. L. Simmons and George J. McCall

Identities and Interactions
Issues in Participant Observation
Social Psychology
Social Research: The Craft of Finding Out

By J. L. Simmons

It's Happening: A Portrait of the Youth Scene Today
Marijuana: Myths and Realities (Editor)
Deviants
The Emerging New Age
Future Lives: A Fearless Guide to Our Transition Times

By George J. McCall

Observing the Law: Field Methods in the Study of Crime and the Criminal Justice System
Social and Structural Factors in Family Violence
The Nursing Assistant's Casebook of Elder Care (with George H. Weber)

76 Ways to Protect Your Child from Crime

■ J. L. Simmons, Ph. D., and
■ George J. McCall, Ph. D.

An Owl Book

Henry Holt and Company
New York

Important Notice

While every effort has been made to provide accurate information and effective crime avoidance tactics, no guarantees of safety can be made by the authors or publisher. Responsibility for the use of the material in this book rests solely with the reader.

Published by Henry Holt and Company, Inc.,
115 West 18th Street, New York, New York 10011.
Published in Canada by Fitzhenry & Whiteside Limited,
91 Granton Drive, Richmond Hill, Ontario L4B 2N5.

Library of Congress Cataloging-in-Publication Data

Simmons, J. L. (Jerry Laird).
76 ways to protect your child from crime / by J. L. Simmons and
George J. McCall. — 1st ed.
p. cm.
"An Owl book."
Includes bibliographical references.
1. Children—United States—Crimes against. 2. Crime prevention—
United States. 3. Child abuse—United States—Prevention.
4. Children and strangers. I. McCall, George J. II. Title.
III. Title: Seventy-six ways to protect your child from crime.
HV6250.4.C48S56 1992 92-13171
649′.1—dc20 CIP
ISBN 0-8050-2071-3 (alk. paper)

Henry Holt books are available at special discounts
for bulk purchases for sales promotions, premiums,
fund-raising, or educational use. Special editions
or book excerpts can also be created to specification.
For details contact: Special Sales Director,
Henry Holt and Company, Inc., 115 West 18th Street,
New York, New York 10011.

First Edition—1992

Designed by Kate Nichols

Printed in the United States of America
Recognizing the importance of preserving the written word,
Henry Holt and Company, Inc., by policy, prints all of its
first editions on acid-free paper. ∞

10 9 8 7 6 5 4 3 2 1

To all the people—the cops, the teachers, the social workers, the volunteers, and all the rest—who strive each day to make the world a safer, better place for kids. They are often overworked and underpaid, and the daily tasks they face sometimes seem insurmountable. But think what a terrible place for children the world would be without them.

And to all the parents who have put their courage and their hearts on the line by bearing and raising children in a sometimes uncertain world.

Contents

Acknowledgments **xi**

Foreword **xiii**

Introduction: The Good News About Children and Crime **1**

1: Raising Crimeproof Kids **5**

#1 Realize You Are Not Alone **6**

#2 How Crimeproofing Tactics Work **8**

#3 Learning from the Bad Guys **10**

#4 Children See—Children Do **13**

#5 Bridging the Generation Gap **14**

#6 Child Protection Networking **16**

#7 Damage Control **18**

2: The Seven Crimeproofing Mega-Strategies **20**

#8 Mega-Strategy One: Keep in Touch **21**

#9 Mega-Strategy Two: Teach Your Children Well **23**

#10 *Mega-Strategy Three: Close and Lock* **26**
#11 *Mega-Strategy Four: Go Public* **27**
#12 *Mega-Strategy Five: Pick Your Spots* **28**
#13 *Mega-Strategy Six: Check It Out* **29**
#14 *Mega-Strategy Seven: Get Along* **30**

3: Creating a Home Security Umbrella **32**

#15 *Choosing Where to Live* **33**
#16 *Crimeproofing Your Dwelling's Exterior* **35**
#17 *Securing Doors and Windows* **37**
#18 *Screening Callers* **40**
#19 *Lights On* **42**
#20 *Security Alarms* **43**
#21 *Children and Telephones* **45**
#22 *Mailbox Security* **48**
#23 *Getting a Family Dog* **49**
#24 *The Gun Gamble* **50**
#25 *What to Do About Intruders* **53**
#26 *Visitors—Friend or Foe* **56**
#27 *Choosing Baby-sitters* **58**
#28 *Safely Home Alone* **60**
#29 *A Neighborhood Safety Net* **63**
#30 *Tell the Police* **65**
#31 *Dealing with Domestic Violence* **67**
#32 *Moving to a New Place* **70**

4: Going Out Safely with Kids **71**

#33 *Staying Together and Staying Public* **72**
#34 *Car Security* **74**

#35 *What to Do If Stranded* 77
#36 *Restroom Safety* 80
#37 *On the Spot: Dealing with Robbery* 82
#38 *Surviving Street Violence* 84
#39 *Professional Services and Disservices* 87
#40 *Family Trips* 90
#41 *Foreign Travel Security* 92

5: Out on Their Own 95

#42 *Help Me!* 96
#43 *Dealing with Strangers* 98
#44 *Out to Play* 100
#45 *Going to and from . . .* 103
#46 *Choosing Day Care and Preschool* 106
#47 *School Security Tips* 108
#48 *School Buses and Mass Transportation* 111
#49 *Bicycle Security* 113
#50 *Malls, Movies, and Munchies* 116
#51 *Halloween* 118
#52 *"Latchkey Kid" Security* 120
#53 *Missing Child* 124
#54 *Preventing Child Molestation and Abuse* 126

6: Teenage Tremors 130

#55 *Keeping the Line Open* 131
#56 *Peer Pressure—The Hidden Persuaders* 134
#57 *Older Companions* 137

#58 *Forbid Hitchhiking* **140**
#59 *Teen Hangout Safety* **142**
#60 *Getting into Mischief* **144**
#61 *Sex—PG, R, and X-Rated* **146**
#62 *Sexual Harassment* **149**
#63 *Avoiding Date Rape* **152**
#64 *Preventing Forcible Rape* **157**
#65 *What to Do If Rape Occurs* **160**
#66 *Dealing with Drugs* **163**
#67 *Curbing Teen Drinking* **168**
#68 *Party Advisories* **171**
#69 *Morbid Moods* **173**
#70 *Avoiding Assault and Murder* **175**
#71 *Securing Money and Valuables* **178**
#72 *Avoiding Scams* **181**
#73 *Part-time Job Security* **183**
#74 *Dealing with Gangs* **186**
#75 *Preventing Runaways* **189**
#76 *Dodging Cults* **192**

Epilogue: Leaving the Nest **195**

Appendix: Where to Get Help **197**

Selected Bibliography **205**

Acknowledgments

This book would be far less without the thousand-and-one contributions of Nola Simmons. Her help in research, in text suggestions, in editing, and in creating the physical manuscript in its many incarnations rises far above "assistance." She is in truth a coauthor.

The painstaking labors of our agents, Michael Larsen and Elizabeth Pomada, have earned our gratitude and hugs.

Theresa Burns, our editor at Henry Holt, deserves bouquets for her unflagging support and countless contributions to the entire project.

We also gratefully thank the exacting and inspiring assistance of our copy editor, Debra Manette, and our production editor, Sabrina Soares.

Finally, we wish to thank the multitude of researchers, practitioners, and investigative journalists who produced the raw materials that have provided the foundation for so much of the book. Without the job they've done, our job would not have been possible.

Foreword

In recent years, crimes against children have escalated dramatically in this country. The faces of missing children from toddlers to teenagers stare at us from milk cartons and fliers posted in windows and on utility poles. Networks of organizations stretch nationwide to help with the desperate efforts of parents to locate young victims of kidnappings and murders. Tenderloin streets and park encampments are filled with kids who were tricked by con artists and drug dealers into believing that life improves with a needle, a liquid, or a powder—that things are best *away* from home.

Our children are in jeopardy today of becoming victims of crime as never before. But there are two indispensable elements to every criminal act: One is the *desire* to commit a crime, the other is the *opportunity*. If either ingredient is missing, a crime can be averted.

This brief but important book spells out the ways you can eliminate the opportunity for a criminal to take advantage of your child. As such, it is a must read for every parent and teacher in America.

We live in a violent society. And, unfortunately, the effectiveness of our criminal justice system is limited. The number of criminals caught, prosecuted, and taken out of circulation will never eliminate the threat to our children. It is, therefore, up to us as adults, parents, teachers, and caregivers, to utilize the tools available to safeguard our children, and, even more important, *to teach them to protect themselves.*

For decades, as San Francisco Police Chief and Police Commissioner—but especially as a parent and grandparent—I have been urging my own family, friends, and the public to recognize the dangers of being young in our society, and to take the very same preventive steps outlined in this book to minimize the risk of children becoming victims of crime. *76 Ways to Protect Your Child from Crime* contains a comprehensive blueprint to guard against becoming such a victim. If you have a child, it is probably the most important book you'll ever acquire at any price.

—Alfred J. Nelder,
Former San Francisco Chief of Police
and Police Commissioner
May 1992

INTRODUCTION

The Good News About Children and Crime

The *Reader's Digest* humorist Lionel Kaufman once remarked: "Children are a great comfort in your old age—and they help you reach it faster too." One source of wrinkles and gray hair for parents is the worry that their kids will be victimized in one way or another by crime.

The ceaseless flood of grim news stories about all the things happening to our youngsters, crimewise, is enough to give any parent a touch of paranoia. We are treated to nightmarish incidents and despairing statistics on how toddlers, urchins, teenagers, and youths fresh from the nest are at risk of being in crime's way.

Yet *tens of millions* of children have grown up, virtually crime free, with only a few scrapes and misadventures along the way. In no way is this just the luck of the draw. It is the direct result of the crime-avoidance and crime-thwarting actions taken by the parents and their children. So there is *good* news about crime.

The statistics from the FBI's infamous Crime Clock are widely publicized. Somewhere in the United States, there is a murder every twenty-six minutes, a forcible rape every six minutes, and a burglary every ten seconds. But there is another statistic that is far more important for our purposes: *Several thousand times every second, someone takes effective action to prevent the crime victimization of a child from happening.*

76 Ways to Protect Your Child from Crime lays out the proven, streetwise tactics for helping you crimeproof your kids. Simply by taking certain steps and training your youngsters to follow certain security habits, the risk factors for all types of child victimization can be reduced to as little as one-tenth the going rates. And in some types of crime, risks can be reduced almost to the vanishing point. Because we are dealing with the ventures and misadventures of life, there can be no 100 percent guarantees. But the child protection principles presented here have proven successful in countless situations. And as a bonus, many of the tips will increase the security of your entire family. So the book is full of good news about raising crime-free kids.

Following the strategies in this book can help keep children out of crime's way in three important ways:

1. The risks of their being victimized by any type of crime will be reduced drastically.
2. You will learn how to prevent them from drifting into criminality themselves.
3. The entire family's security will be increased, so the kids don't become victims by default.

We deal mainly with the first two of these factors. But as you apply the strategies, your own security will automatically increase as well. Use the tactics yourself, when *you* travel to and from a night-school class or go out to play. If this book saves you and your family from even one minor incident, it will have been more than worth your time and the cover price.

You *can* change the odds against crime. And you can do so without having to adopt a garrison mentality where your family crouches within a fortress and resigns from living. By changing the odds, you change the course of your children's lives.

Even though the book's entries are by the numbers, addressing different situations, they weave together to form a holistic security pattern in which the pointers supplement and reinforce each other. Some steps involve establishing and maintaining a security umbrella over the kids. Others involve teaching your youngsters some crime-avoidance habits and skills. Some involve more subtle interpersonal factors. Many tactics are distilled from common sense and might even seem simplistic, yet a great many cases show that these were often the ones a crime victim neglected to follow.

Probably no one applies all these tactics unerringly, all the time, in all circumstances. The perfect parent has never existed, nor the perfect child. Do the best you can, knowing that as you incorporate each security measure into your family's life-style, the life-style becomes less and less crime prone.

We suggest that you read through the entire book, picking up pointers and seeing where you may be at risk. Then use it as a reference manual and begin to implement the suggested tactics. The first chapter presents essential data about the current crime scene and kids; the second introduces the seven major generic crime-protection strategies. Chapter 3 outlines the pointers for creating a secure home environment. Chapter 4 addresses going out safely with your youngsters. Chapter 5 shows how you can safeguard kids as they venture out on their own, and chapter 6 details steps for navigating the teen years and dealing with the many situations that might arise. The recommendations might seem a bit repetitive in places because the same tips apply to many different situations. However, these tips are well worth repeating.

This book is based on a great deal of hard-won collective experience of parents, researchers, and practitioners. The tactics are drawn from leading-edge criminology and social psychology researchers, the recommendations of veteran crime-prevention workers, and the in-depth accounts of offenders and victims. We have also personally done a good deal of research, writing, and consulting on crime and deviance. And we have colloborated with our wives in raising two sets of relatively crime-free children. We've gone through the missing bikes and the temporarily missing kids; the petty thefts and intimidations; the awkward silences and anxious hearts—we've been there.

1

Raising Crimeproof Kids

Parenting has been called one of the most important jobs anyone can have, and the one we are often least prepared for. The entries in this chapter lay out essential know-before-you-go information about the crime scene and your children's security.

You are the guardian, the overseer, the teacher, and the facilitator for your children as they grow. The information in this chapter will help you play these roles more effectively and with more assurance.

Realize You Are Not Alone

The thought of your kids being home alone or somewhere out on their own in an uncertain world is enough to create plenty of anxiety. If both you and your spouse work, or if you are a single parent, you sometimes might feel a bit like a refugee struggling somehow to protect your child in a land of lurking dangers. But take heart, because you actually have a great deal of support and assistance.

You are not at all alone in being actively concerned about your children's welfare and protection. Yes, there are some bad guys on the loose out there. Yet there are far more people who mean your children well and who are willing to help extend an umbrella of security over them. Almost any store clerk, police officer, teacher, bus driver, telephone operator, or neighborhood acquaintance will aid them if they are lost or in trouble. There are also several million professionals and active volunteers who are working hard to keep the youth of our society out of crime's way and give them the chance to be all that they can be. For example, NOVA, the National Organization for Victims Assistance, estimates that there are over eight thousand different organizations working to prevent crime victimization and to assist victims. So you can begin to see that you are not on your own in a hostile or uncaring world.

If you currently are going through a serious problem with your children, turn immediately to the "Where to Get Help" section at the back of the book, and reach out and contact someone. Hotlines and support groups have an outstanding record of giving aid and support. And they're just a phone call away.

If your current situation is okay, or only mildly hysterical, read through the pages of this book and begin to apply the principles. They work. And, as you use them, everyone but the bad guys will win.

#2

How Crimeproofing Tactics Work

Crime statistics can be alarming but they can also be very misleading and needlessly frightening. The truth is, virtually no youngsters run the "average" risks. Children's chances of victimization are almost always much less or much greater than these averages, depending on what they and their family do and don't do. This is very good news because, by your own actions, you can drastically change the odds in your children's favor.

Statistics are based on random probabilities, but modern criminologists have found that there is really no such thing as "random" crime. Crime incidents are always a matter of circumstances. *When you change the circumstances, you change the likelihood of a crime happening. This is how prevention tactics work*. For instance, a teenager who stays away from high-crime areas at night will cut the odds of being mugged to maybe one-fifth the average. If teens also go out with companions and stay in public view, they might further cut the odds to one-fifth of that. This means they have cut their chances to one twenty-fifth of the "average" risk.

Whatever a would-be perpetrator might have in mind, there must be both a *target* and an *opportunity* if a crime is to happen. Criminals go for easy targets and pass by the ones that promise more difficulty. For example, an unlocked bicycle left outside probably won't make it through the night, while a chained bike put away in a locked garage probably will. Crimeproofing your kids and their belongings is usually that easy.

One other thing about crime statistics is well worth knowing. While highly publicized by the media, many gruesome and alarming types of crimes against children are actually very rare in most locales. These include kidnapping by strangers, murder, and psychopathic street violence. And some savvy tactics, as we will explain, can reduce the likelihood of these ever happening to you and yours almost to the vanishing point.

#3

Learning from the Bad Guys

One of the first things new recruits in most police academies learn is that there is no such thing as a "criminal type." You can't spot a criminal by his or her looks. Perpetrators can be of any age, ethnic background, sex, appearance, or station in life. There are devoutly religious child molesters and tough young punks who protect little kids from harm.

We really don't know what causes crime, even after two centuries of intensive research and theorizing. Biological, psychological, sociological, economic, and moral theories have all been advanced. But while each of these theories explains some cases, none of them even begins to explain all crime.

The theories haven't been of too much use, but crime research has given us a wealth of findings that can be applied directly to crime avoidance. For instance, we now know that child molesters scan playgrounds looking for the lone child whose body language suggests he or she might be vulnerable. We know that cities with populations under fifty thousand have far lower crime rates than giant metropolises, and that within big cities, most street crime is confined to certain districts. We know that the majority of rapes occur Friday and Saturday nights between 10 P.M. and 4 A.M. We know that most muggers don't injure their victims unless the victims resist. We know that burglars are much less interested in hitting on houses where there is an alarm system or a dog. These and similar findings can be translated directly into effective crimeproofing tactics. Learning about how criminals operate can tell you how to avoid and thwart them.

There are three main categories of offenders. The highly skilled professionals are only a tiny fraction of the criminal element, and they usually have no interest in children. (Even most hardened criminals despise child molesters.) Semiskilled habitual lawbreakers, a much larger group, usually have halfway effective crime techniques worked out, although these criminals are seldom successful in the long run. They are usually, but not always, young, male, and inner-city residents. They are often known to the police and may already have a record. Their chances of being arrested for any single crime are not great, but their chance of eventually being imprisoned is very high. Their lives tend to be unstable, and the majority leave a life of crime behind as they grow older. Many of the steps in the following pages are designed to keep your children (and you) out of their way.

By far the largest number of perpetrators are amateurs, and this is good news because they are the most easily thwarted. Locked doors, your youngsters staying in public view, and a few commonsense precautions are usually sufficient to deter them.

Criminals look for easy targets. This is the key thing to know about them. They are observers—sometimes keen ones. Based on their observations, they judge how easy or difficult a potential target might be, and then they act or don't act accordingly. Almost all would-be perpetrators shun situations that promise to be difficult or a hassle of some kind.

Without ever intending to, kids and parents sometimes "cooperate" with offenders by neglecting simple security tactics. Criminals play the odds too. Burglars know that if they check out enough houses, they'll find one with an unlocked garage door or open basement window. Would-be molesters know that if they wait, they'll find a lone child taking a shortcut through an isolated area. And young amateur drug dealers know there will be some emotionally vulnerable teenagers who will buy their wares. But by following the security guidelines, you can help see to it that your kids do not cooperate unwittingly.

There is a widespread myth about criminals that needs to be exploded. For decades now, they have been romanticized in story and song. There have been many sympathetic dramas about western outlaws, Mafia bosses, teenage gang lords, prostitutes, and misunderstood delinquents. But the actual truth is that criminals are about as glamorous as a backed-up sewer. Crime and fear of crime impoverish everyone's life. Perpetrators are willing to exploit and brutalize anyone for their own selfish purposes, and they lose no sleep over the plight of their victims. There is little that is admirable or honorable about them, and they are good friends to no one. When caught, they routinely turn against each other to get lighter sentences. They also sometimes try to justify their actions by pointing to their economically impoverished backgrounds or dysfunctional upbringing. Yet millions of other people have had tough lives without resorting to mugging or molesting their fellow human beings. Even if you or your children are careless and something happens, always remember you and yours are not the ones to blame—the perpetrator is the culprit.

#4

Children See — Children Do

James Baldwin, the eminent American writer, once remarked that children don't listen to their parents but they surely do imitate them. Children are peerless copycats. The sometimes unsettling truth is that we are on display to our children, and they pick up far more from us than we are usually aware of.

The work of family therapists such as Alice Miller and John Bradshaw amply demonstrates that parents influence their kids far more extensively and deeply than they usually realize. This might make you feel a bit self-conscious, but it also gives you the opportunities for crimeproofing your kids.

As children see you practicing good security measures, they will begin to pick them up almost automatically. This isn't all there is to protecting children, but it lays a very good foundation. Because children are such good mimics, your own security habits serve the double functions of providing immediate family protection and giving your child security training by your own example. If you routinely lock up and check to see who's there before opening the front door, for instance, your kids probably will adopt these habits just as "the way things are."

There's another thing about children's mimicry to keep in mind. If you have "bad habits" that you don't want your kids to copy—such as recreational substance abuse or adventurous liaisons—you might want to consider changing them. At the very least, indulge in them away from your youngsters' presence. Yes, you have your own life to lead. And living only for your children can be unhealthy for everyone concerned. Without getting into self-blame look over your own behavior and see what you *don't* want your kids to pick up.

#5

Bridging the Generation Gap

Times have changed.

Parents remember the way things were while they were growing up, but their children are growing up in a different world. All the differences between *then* and *now* virtually guarantee some generation gap. (You might recall experiencing something of the sort with your own parents.)

Generation gaps create psychological distancing and often some alienation between parents and kids, so they can breed conflicts that impede protection from crime. Some bridging efforts are therefore in order.

It is necessary to be at least somewhat in tune with the times in order to guard your kids successfully. Many of the changes that have come along have been good. There are new careers and opportunities, fewer tooth cavities and longer life expectancies. But crime has increased, along with the technical wonders and longer life spans. For instance, it might have been perfectly safe for you to stroll in the park or on the beach by yourself years ago, but not today. On the other hand, you might overreact to your children's adulation of some rock star prancing around in her underwear.

Your children are also very likely to test your limits as they innocently reflect the world they find—such as the preteen who bounced up to her mother one day and asked: "Mom, did you masturbate when you were a schoolgirl?"

Most parent-child relationships weather a generation gap and survive. Perhaps the best advice comes from the wife of evangelist Billy Graham. When asked about raising her own children, she answered, "Just pray for a thick skin and a tender heart."

It is good to keep in mind that you and your youngsters are *not equal* in knowledge and experience. No matter how bright they may be, they are far more naive than you, and they'll remain so—at least well into their teens. You'll need to listen to them and they'll need to listen to you.

#6

Child Protection Networking

According to anthropologists, neighbors watching out for each other is the most ancient form of crime control. It was the standard practice in most "primitive" cultures, and their crime rates were almost always much lower than ours are. Next to your own personal security habits, a mutual-aid security network is still the most effective crime-control approach—far more effective than crackdown legislation or wars on crime declared by politicians. Even just maintaining a stable, kept-up neighborhood has proven to be crime resistive; research has shown that crime rates are highest in rundown locales filled with transients and strangers.

There is nothing mysterious about a network. It can be as simple as getting together with two or three other closeby families and working out a few informal agreements, such as: "Let's watch out for each other's kids, and if they get in trouble they can stop at our house." Then you can build up from there. You don't have to become pals with your neighbors, or even like them particularly, and they might not agree with your politics or life-style. But it's important to know who they are and to develop a united front against criminal intrusions.

You will find if you casually ask that most other people, especially the ones with children, are vitally interested in security. Even the people around you *without* kids can be interested and mobilized with little trouble.

Besides increased security, social researchers have found that even rudimentary networks can have a host of other benefits. Networks can be a source of companionship; emotional support;

jobs; baby-sitters; referrals to mechanics, dentists, and other professionals; and even dates and spouses. Other parents, who are in something of the same boat, are particularly helpful, as you share many vital interests with them.

It is important to include the local police and other community authorities in your network if at all possible. Police scandals and abuses have received a lot of coverage in recent years. But these stories entirely miss the fact that police officers help thousands of people daily and save thousands of lives each year. If your youngsters or you are in a tight situation of some sort, whom would you most like to see show up?

#7

Damage Control

A widely quoted epigram runs: "Life is something that happens to you while you are making other plans." This is certainly true when it involves our children being victimized, even when the victimization is "minor." While victimization is an uncomfortable subject, it needs to be looked in the eye.

Probably no children have ever lived who have not collected a few emotional and physical scrapes while growing up. If there are such people, the authors have never met or heard of them. If your youngsters have something stolen, are taunted and humiliated, are sexually molested or beaten up, you naturally are going to be upset. For what it's worth, hundreds of millions of people throughout the world—both parents and children—have survived such incidents and gone on in spite of this to build successful lives. This fact is a testimonial to the resilience of the human spirit.

As a parent you have a twofold aim: to minimize the occurrence of such incidents and to minimize the damage if they *do* occur. If something does happen, you'll want to help youngsters handle it and minimize the aftereffects.

There is a saying in counseling centers that all trainee therapists, when they start out, talk too much and listen too little. As a parent, it is understandable if you get upset and start talking when your children encounter crime. But in almost all cases, the most important thing you can do for the children is to *listen.* The youngsters are already going through emotional aftershocks. It is *crucial* not to add to the children's pain and confusion. Therapy patients sometimes recount that when they were young, they had to deal not only with a childhood trauma, but also with the trauma of their family's angry and accusing reactions.

Get the children to talk about fears or the incident so it doesn't become bottled up inside. Try your best to listen without judgment, blame, or recrimination. Research has shown this to be the most crucial factor in recovery. Unless the situation makes it absolutely necessary, give only the advice and help that is asked for. Don't force children to do something they are afraid to do, unless you have to for medical or other pressing reasons.

Comfort the children. They'll need a hug and some support far more than a lecture. And, as soon as you get a chance, talk out your own feelings about the incident with a good listener.

What if your children have done something criminal? Apply discipline, of course, but as calmly as you can, not vindictively. Otherwise, follow the same rules of hearing the children out and providing support. One of the main traits of healthy families is mutual support of its members.

Whatever has happened, don't encourage children to be victims. Melodie Beatie, Wayne Dyer, John Bradshaw, and a host of other experts have emphasized that accepting the role of victim is a terrible habit to fall into because it keeps the upset alive in the mind and heart. The renowned humanist-doctor Bernie Siegel strongly advises patients with life-threatening diseases to think of themselves as *survivors*, not victims. This is good advice for crime victims too.

You may be surprised sometimes by how deeply hurt children are by some incident that seems minor to you. A stolen toy might be as heartbreaking to a child as a stolen car would be to you. On the other hand, with our own children, we found that we were sometimes much more upset than the kids were.

Whatever happens, help your children come to the realization that it is not the end of the world. Given half a chance, kids have an astonishing ability to bounce back and recover even from horrendous incidents.

2

The Seven Crimeproofing Mega-Strategies

The entries in this chapter introduce the seven most important, generic, bottom-line strategies for crimeproofing your kids. The beauty of these strategies is that they are mutually reinforcing; they work together to form an overall holistic safety net. They are also timeless—they were effective decades ago and they will be effective in the decades to come.

We recently examined all the serious crime stories reported in one month's worth of a major daily metropolitan newspaper (the St. Louis *Post-Dispatch*). And we found that, even with only the sketchy details provided, in over 90 percent of the cases one or more of these crimeproofing principles were violated.

We introduce each strategy in turn, but here is a master checklist.

Mega-Strategy One: *Keep in Touch*
Mega-Strategy Two: *Teach Your Children Well*
Mega-Strategy Three: *Close and Lock*
Mega-Strategy Four: *Go Public*
Mega-Strategy Five: *Pick Your Spots*
Mega-Strategy Six: *Check It Out*
Mega-Strategy Seven: *Get Along*

Mega-Strategy One: Keep in Touch

The more in touch you are with your youngsters, the less likely they are to get into crime's way.

Being in touch has several aspects. It involves knowing where your children are and what they are up to. *Some* degree of keeping track of and supervising your kids is necessary until they are old enough to leave the nest. Otherwise, you literally lose track of them.

Being in touch also involves maintaining an open, two-way flow of communication. The importance of open parent-child communication can't be overemphasized. Children will never tell you everything, but they should be able to tell you anything if they need to.

Crimewise, you need two things from this open communication line: information (What's going on?) and feelings (How do you feel about it?). If you know these two things on a regular basis, you are much more able to take effective action when problems arise. If your kids are being hassled or hustled, you need to hear about it.

A full rundown of communication skills goes beyond the scope of this book, but here are a few pointers that can make a lot of difference.

First, talk to your children about anything, little things, it doesn't matter much what; the point is sharing communication. Second, *listen* to what they say respectfully. Work on developing basic listening skills. As they start to express themselves, no matter how outlandishly, hear them out, without interrupting, judging, or advising. This is fairly easy to explain but not always easy to do, and some lapses will be inevitable. After they've had their say, *then* you can say, "Well, I think maybe . . ." or whatever. This simple procedure may open up your communication lines beyond belief. And you'll know a lot more about what's going on with your children, including any danger signals. You also will be much more likely to sense early on if youngsters are drifting toward criminality.

Never belittle or laugh at a child's thoughts, feelings, and fears. Children's feelings are easily hurt, as you may well remember from your own childhood. Laughing at children's feelings breaks down what counselors call the "interpersonal bridge" between you and them, and they'll go silent or go elsewhere to talk. No living, breathing parent (or child) lives up to these pointers all the time, but this is something to work toward. If more people could just learn to *listen* nonjudgmentally, half the family problems of the world might be resolved.

Allow your children to have opinions that differ from yours—they will anyway. When you allow it, you encourage more open communication. And try to be a parent who is "askable."

Keeping in touch also means not hiding yourself away from them. Both you and they should, ideally, be able to express the full range of emotions safely. To the extent that you can be open with them mentally and emotionally, they will learn from you, and they won't have to spend months or years with a therapist later in life, learning how to feel and express themselves. Also, they will be much less likely to substitute addictions for living.

A caution—don't dump all the gory details of your troubles on them, such as a financial crisis or your marital upsets, because they are in no place to help handle it. You can say, "We need to tighten our belts for a bit," or some such, without all the confusing details.

We have much more to say about keeping in touch in other sections.

#9

Mega-Strategy Two: Teach Your Children Well

No parents have ever been able to be with their children all of the time. Because of modern life-styles, where both parents work or a single parent is raising youngsters, this is even more true today. But your *training* can be with your children all the time—through their whole lives.

Parents sense that times have changed, and this awareness is reflected in international opinion polls. Half a century ago, the quality parents valued most in children was obedience. But in the last few decades there has been a dramatic shift toward valuing self-reliance and independence. In part, this is a direct response to the changes in modern living conditions. Youngsters are now more often out on their own or home alone. Today children need to learn crime-avoidance habits right along with toilet training, grooming, and tying shoes. So how is this teaching best done?

First off, by your own good example. As your children see you applying security tactics, they will pick up on them and make them their own. For instance, when they see that you always lock the car door or always refuse a second drink, they'll probably grow up doing the same things.

Beyond your own example, give them hands-on practice in security habits just as soon as they are old enough. Let them check and lock all the doors, see that the windows are shut, turn on a downstairs light, lock up their outside toys. Don't do it all for them or they won't learn to do it themselves, and they will (probably wrongly) expect it to be done for them as they grow older.

Be patient in your teaching so youngsters have a safe, supportive environment to learn in. For the sake of family security you'll need to "check their work" for a while, of course. Praise them when they get it right. And when correcting, correct the action, don't criticize the child.

Don't just tell them what to do; help them be able to do it. Showing is better than telling because it involves more of a child's entire motor and sensory systems and both hemispheres of the brain, as cutting-edge learning researchers have found. Think of your training not as lecturing and admonishing, but as an apprenticeship—you are apprenticing your kids in keeping themselves (and you) safe. As with the learning of any human skill, repetitive instruction and practice are the keys to success.

Finally, there are verbal instructions and rehearsals. One excellent form of these is "what-if" role-playing games, highly recommended by child safety experts. Its form is a simple game. "What if a stranger pulls up and offers you candy?" "What if someone comes to the door and wants to use our phone?" "What if a bigger kid demands your lunch money?" "What if we get separated at the mall?" Such games rehearse actual situations children might encounter, so that they have looked at possible options and, with your help, picked out effective ones. They're then less likely to be caught off guard.

Apprenticing and role-playing situations teach children confidence and competence, whereas dire admonitions are more likely just to scare them. Remember that you are not just training children for that afternoon or the route to school. You are helping forge lifetime skills.

Verbal instructions will help and are necessary because you can't supply "real-life" handling of such things as a mugging or an eruption of street violence. But keep in mind that the understanding level of youngsters is very incomplete and often distorted. For instance, a five-year-old boy solemnly told the authors that a bad person was someone who "went pooh in his pants." Another boy thought school was a place you were sent for punishment if you acted up. And a young girl pronounced that men who broke into houses and took things should be spanked.

So be concrete and action-focused in your training, especially with young children. Emphasize what they can *do*, not what is scary. This increases their sense of mastery and reduces fears.

#10

Mega-Strategy Three: Close and Lock

It is amazing, but over one-third of all property crimes, and many crimes against kids and parents, result from carelessness about closing and locking doors and windows. This carelessness gives perpetrators the chance that otherwise wouldn't exist. As we have said before, only a small fraction of offenders will go to much trouble to score; easy targets are their meat. *So any actions that increase their difficulty are effective*.

People often keep their front doors and driver's side doors locked or chain up their bikes when they are through riding. Where they usually fall down is neglecting other potential entrances or not bothering to lock the car or bike when they make quick stops. The basement window needs closing, the garage door needs locking, the window onto the patio needs securing too. The passenger door needs to be locked at all times and the bike needs to be locked even when you just "run in for a minute." Closing and locking should be inflexible habits even if a friend says, "Oh, don't worry, it's safe around here." Unlocked possessions or potential entries are simply an invitation, while routinely closing and locking is especially effective against amateurs, who are the largest percentage of offenders. Specific tips on how and when to close and lock are covered in chapters 3, 4, and 5.

It is vital to train your kids early and well about closing and locking, because they tend to run in and out so much. Otherwise, their negligence produces unwitting breaches in your family security.

#11

Mega-Strategy Four: Go Public

Around two-thirds of all crimes against children (and adults) happen when they are (1) alone and (2) isolated from public view. Two people, even children, are far more than twice as safe as one. Staying near populated areas and away from isolated spots further increases a youngster's security level.

Kids who go to the park or the mall alone are much more at risk than kids who go with others. And kids who explore deserted buildings on their own or take secluded shortcuts after dark are tipping the odds against themselves.

Almost all criminals try to avoid being seen and identified publicly. That fact can be turned into one of the most effective defenses against crime for children and grown-ups alike.

When two or more people are together, perpetrators are also likely to pass them by because of the greatly increased potential complications. A habitual mugger put it simply: "One person . . . maybe; two people, no way."

Crime incidents sometimes do happen where there are large crowds, such as at a rock concert or busy mall. But in most such cases, the victim either went alone or neglected other major protection strategies.

Going public and staying in public view deters virtually every type of crime. If a child is threatened or in trouble, getting near other people is also the simplest, most effective action to take. Teach your children this mega-strategy thoroughly—verbally, through hands-on apprenticing, and by your own example.

#12

Mega-Strategy Five: Pick Your Spots

Crime risks of all types are far greater in certain locations, at certain times, and under certain circumstances than others. So where you live and where and when you go out with youngsters can make all the difference. For instance, in a large city, some districts may have crime rates as much as *twenty times higher* than other districts. And even in these districts, rates might be five times as high on a weekend evening as on a weekday morning.

The spots where you park and the spots where children play or jog or stop for a treat have important security implications. Part of being "streetwise" is learning to distinguish between safe and unsafe circumstances.

Having to avoid certain times and places, and making your kids do so too, might seem like a curtailment of your basic human rights. And perhaps it is. But doing so is realistic and prudent, the equivalent of taking extra precautions in stormy weather.

If you do need or wish to go into less safe areas, abiding by the other strategies will greatly reduce your risks. For instance, if your youngsters' dentist is located in a deteriorating inner-city area, pick the safer early times of day, go along with them, and park in a populated area close to the entrance.

The relative safety of various locations and situations also changes over time. Beaches and parks are now not so safe, and some colorful neighborhoods have become mean streets. You should be alert to signs of such changes.

The chapters that follow give many specific pointers on *how* to pick your spots.

#13

Mega-Strategy Six: Check It Out

Checking it out—whatever it is—has been a mainstay strategy of the wise since time immemorial. In fact, it is a survival trait we share with the animal kingdom. Watch a cat or bird scanning its environment and making a continuous series of judgment calls about security in response.

You should apply this generic strategy to everything from your children's new friend, to a school rumor, to a recommended medical treatment, to a new romantic interest of your own, to moving into new quarters.

Checking it out entails a deliberate and sometimes thorough "look before you leap." We all usually do best when we are private investigators to some degree. You shouldn't just leave things to chance or the possibly self-serving recommendations of some professional.

Checking it out also involves developing and tuning into a subtle discernment, intuition, or "sixth sense" about what is safe and when it is time to go. Again and again, victims report "they had a feeling" they should have left the party early or shouldn't have gone down that street, but they went ahead. No one has come up with a satisfactory explanation of this sixth sense. But experts suggest it involves being alert and paying attention to current surroundings, being wary of anything that seems out of place, and listening to inner promptings. Evidently, training enhances it too.

Checking it out might also involve no more than taking the trouble to make some phone calls, for example, about a potential preschool or a party your youngsters are invited to.

#14

Mega-Strategy Seven: Get Along

It has been said that good manners provide the lubricant that keeps social life working. It is certainly true that for crime avoidance, getting along with others is as important as locking your doors. For example, disagreements and arguments are the cause of a large proportion of aggravated assaults among both minors and adults. In many cases the victim was even the first aggressor. Investigations have shown that many instances of harassment, petty theft, and vandalism were related to "getting even."

It is important to teach children not to create ill will needlessly, because criminal acts, from bullying to murder, often reflect this even-the-score vengefulness. Even your idle conversational style can influence your likelihood of being assaulted.

There are many ways to get along interpersonally without being wimpy, and it is a very good idea to train your children in some of them. Besides crime avoidance, they have lots of other positive win-friends-and-influence-people effects. People come out better, whatever they are doing, when they are surrounded by goodwill rather than ill will.

You can usually short-circuit a tricky situation by just refusing to escalate it. As Joe McNamara, a former San Jose police chief, suggests: "Be a coward and go home."

Children from toddlers to youths are notoriously fickle in their alliances and disputes. Yet the practice of a few interpersonal skills can save them grief. For instance, communication experts recommend making "I statements" instead of "you statements." ("I'm angry," rather than "You piss me off.") You statements are always at least implicitly accusative and provoking.

Getting along also involves saying no firmly, but diplomatically with perhaps a plausible reason why, so you don't create any rancor.

Youngsters should learn not to make jokes at others' expense, because the people they taunt and belittle will take it *very* personally, and who knows what vengeance they may concoct in their hearts? And if someone else taunts your kids, they really don't have to pick up the gauntlet.

Body language can be important. An open-handed, open-faced posture is friendly, while a leaning-forward, frowning one can be provoking. Humor that is not at someone else's expense can often defuse a situation.

Crime researchers have found something called "victim prones," similar to the insurance companies' discovery of "accident prones." Some people repeatedly are crime victims while others are never victimized. Getting-along skills are a major effective strategy for avoiding such proneness.

It is also useful to teach youngsters about win-win interpersonal strategies, scenarios where everybody involved wins, at least to some extent. Trying to see the other person's viewpoint and taking it into account can defuse many interpersonal situations. Favoring and pursuing win-win activities builds up a person's interpersonal goodwill "bank account," which can make the difference when the chips are down.

As we said before, there can be no absolute guarantees. But, whatever your local crime conditions might be, these seven generic strategies can weave together and augment one another to produce greatly increased security for your kids.

The next four chapters provide specific applications of these seven mega-strategies.

3

Creating a Home Security Umbrella

Modern Nobel physicists tell us that we don't just experience reality—we help create it. The entries in this chapter detail steps for creating a much more secure home-life environment for children to grow up within.

You can never just presume that the police and other authorities are providing all the security your family needs. They are overworked and budget-hassled and can't be everywhere at once. Security is always in your own hands to some extent.

Parents are, among so many other things, the guardians of the next generation. The mostly simple steps that follow will aid in that guardianship.

#15

Choosing Where to Live

Decade after decade, FBI and Justice Department statistics provide massive documentation of the fact that *where* you live is one of the most important and enduring factors influencing risks of all types of crime. In truth, it is probably the most important single factor, so thoroughly checking out the place you choose to live is worthwhile.

As a general rule, the smaller the community, the safer it is. For instance, cities of under fifty thousand people are, overall, more than twice as free of almost all types of crime as huge metropolitan areas. Within cities of any size, certain districts or neighborhoods are far safer than others. This means you *can* live in a metropolitan area if you pick your spots with care and knowledge.

In choosing where to live, no doubt you will pay some attention to schools, shopping, and convenience of location. But you want to pay at least as much attention to the crime situation. Talk with a number of people living in the area—some residents and shopkeepers—and pay special attention to how they *feel* about living and working there. Walk into the local police precinct and ask the officers on duty about the area. Drive slowly around the streets at different times of the day and night, if you can.

One of the most reliable indications of how crime-ridden the locale might be is how well it is kept up. Are houses and buildings in good repair, with no broken windows and abandoned dwellings? Are the streets and lawns well kept up or deteriorating? These physical signs are one of the best barometers of the quality of life in a neighborhood.

How much turnover of residency is there? Areas with low turnover rates are usually also low-crime neighborhoods.

Do the people on the streets appear cheerful or sullen? The neighborhood does not have to be an expensive upper-middle-class one to be stable and relatively crime free. Many locales with a mix of working-class people and retirees are pretty secure.

Rentals and real estate prices are usually much lower in high-crime or unstable transition areas, but they may be no bargain at all. Prices also are usually much lower in small-town and semirural areas, which are often some of the safest places in the nation. If you *must* live in a risky area, you still can greatly enhance your family's security by following the tips in the remainder of this chapter. But in most ways you are much better off with modest quarters in a low-crime area rather than more room and ambience in a high-crime one.

If you are raising your kids in a neighborhood that is beginning to deteriorate seriously, you have two rational choices: (1) Get together pronto with neighbors, the police, and local leaders to take vigorous concerted action to reverse the trend; or (2) move. Don't just hope it will all somehow come out okay.

If you are a single working parent, and especially if your kids are a bit older now, you might consider an apartment or condo complex. But don't just accept the assurances of managers or real estate agents; do your own checking.

Incidentally, research data show that most burglars strike within six blocks of where they themselves live.

#16

Crimeproofing Your Dwelling's Exterior

The more secure your dwelling is, the more secure your children are from every type of crime. The exterior and grounds are the gateways between your home and the outside world. A security umbrella therefore starts with your dwelling's exterior.

We've already noted that criminals are usually keen observers. Some are coldly calculating, and some just go on gut feelings. But all of them, whatever their intentions, screen dwellings to decide how inviting or discouraging they are as possible targets. The details of your dwelling's exterior provide a "first impression" to anyone with trouble in mind.

Walk around the outside of your dwelling, thinking like a would-be intruder. How could *you* get inside? Have a friend or two do the same thing. Do this even if you live in a condo or upper-story apartment. Then do something preventive about whatever security lapses you find.

In doing your inspection, be sure to take into account the fact that most potential intruders are young and agile. Look for balconies, fire escapes, and tall trees. *You* may have given up climbing trees or scurrying up ledges a long time ago, but a youthful burglar may be adept at it. Trim back any tree branches that might provide a pathway into the dwelling. And any upper-story windows or doorways reachable from the ground should be locked securely and routinely.

An important aspect of effective Neighborhood Watch programs is that all dwellings are clearly visible to public view. Landscaping also needs to be done with some attention to crime avoidance. Exterior shrubbery needs to be trimmed so that it is not a potential hiding place for perpetrators. You need a clear, unobstructed path to your entry doors. Often-neglected areas are the sides and back of the dwelling, where tall hedges or untrimmed bushes might provide hiding places. Cut foliage in such a way that it does not obscure exterior lighting. You want a clear view of all your entrances, day and night, so you can easily see from a distance when arriving home if anything is wrong. You also want this clear visibility if young children are playing in the yard.

Always leave a light on inside the house and perhaps a radio tuned low to a talk show while you're away. A dark, quiet house with only an exterior light on is often a signal that no one is home. Teach your kids these elementary habits and show them by doing the routines yourself.

Don't ever leave stepladders outside the dwelling; there's no reason to aid a would-be intruder. Also, don't leave anything outside, such as bikes or lawn mowers, that you don't want stolen. Train your children to help you check over the exterior grounds and secure any neglected items. Children learn security habits best by hands-on participation.

If you live in an apartment complex or a condo, take the time to learn, together with your children, the locations of the entryways, the manager, the security system, and the fire alarms. Teach children to use the fire alarm and yell "Fire!" in case of personal trouble. Even if it turns out to be a false alarm, the extra security is well worth the hassles.

If you and your youngsters arrive home and see any signs of a break-in, *don't go inside*. Go to a neighbor or nearby phone booth and call the police. And keep your children close by you in any such suspected emergency. It is always best to avoid direct confrontation with a perpetrator if you can.

The essential strategy is to give your dwelling the appearance of being secured and occupied. Taking steps to crimeproof your dwelling exterior is a very effective beginning.

#17

Securing Doors and Windows

Would-be perpetrators cannot intrude into your dwelling unless they can find and force their way through some entrance. So it is essential to keep all potential entrances closed and locked even when you are just stepping outside or going over to the neighbors' for a moment.

People often lock their front doors yet are careless about other possible entrances. According to the National Crime Prevention Council, in over *40 percent* of all dwelling robberies, the thieves simply walked in through an unlocked door or crawled through an unlocked window.

One of the things younger children do a lot is run in and out. If you live in a relatively safe locale, this may be no problem during the daytime if you also are home. Most criminals would shun this obvious level of bustling activity, especially if there was a dog around and other neighbors going in and out of their homes. However, soon you may find virtually every potential entry unsecured. Both you and the kids *are* wide open, especially to snatch-and-run hits, if tempting items such as jewelry lying around the house or toys left outside seem easily available.

Locks in older dwellings are often inadequate. Even in new homes and apartments, builders often scrimp on costs by providing good locks on front doors, but only flimsy ones on other entrances, such as the garage door leading into the house. Also, other entryways often have hollow-core doors, which can be kicked in fairly easily.

All crime experts agree that deadbolt locks that extend at

least an inch and a half into the door jamb are best. You can get good deadbolt locks for under $20 at discount hardware stores, and, if you are at all handy, they are easy to install. If you are not handy, you probably have a friend or relative who is. If you live in a condo or apartment complex, the maintenance or security man would probably help you with installation for a few dollars.

Solid wooden doors (under $40) are much more secure than hollow-core ones, so you might consider replacing any of the latter for outside entryways and attached garage-to-house doors. If a door has a glass window in it, consider replacing it or covering the glass on the inside with protective wire mesh.

With sliding glass doors, it's a good idea to install an additional lock, which you can buy for a few dollars at hardware or chain department stores. Also, cut a piece of wood to fit into the bottom runner, which will prevent the door from being opened more than a few inches. Old broom handles, cut to the right length, work wonderfully for this. Do this for any accessible second-story patio or fire escape doors too.

An excellent temporary measure for door security is to pick up rubber doorstops for under a dollar in the houseware section of department stores. A doorstop wedged under the door will strongly reinforce even flimsy doors surprisingly well.

People often overlook the fact that windows should not just be shut *but locked* when not open. Also, if accessible from outside, they should be opened only far enough for ventilation, not far enough to admit a body. You can do this easily with window stops; even a strong nail driven above the bottom sash or a block of wood nailed inside the track will allow ventilation but prevent entry. For easily reached windows, consider additional locks, which are inexpensive. The "butterfly" locks that windows ordinarily come with are not very secure. Needless to say, children need to be taught window security along with locking doors.

Ordinary door chains, while popular, are not very secure because intruders can often throw their weight against one and break it loose. However, this probably can't be done if you have a case-hardened steel chain plus an ordinary rubber doorstop slipped under the inside edge of the door. (Case hardening is a smelting process that produces especially strong and break-resistant steel.)

We've found that prices for security items vary greatly, so comparison shop.

#18

Screening Callers

The vast majority of the people who come to your front door are not dangerous. Many you know. Some have legitimate business, such as the mail carrier or UPS package deliverers; others are bothersome at most. But a tiny minority are not so wholesome. So you and your kids have a basic screening job. And the inflexible bottom-line rule is: *Don't let unsolicited strangers into your home*.

One of your best security investments is a wide-angle peephole lens in your front door. These are inexpensive and easily installed, and you can see who is at the door without opening it. If someone you don't know comes to another entrance, ask him to come around to the front.

If someone comes to your door claiming to be from an agency or company and you are even vaguely suspicious, ask him to wait and make a call to verify his authenticity. (The same would apply for unrecognized women callers because they are frequently partners in dwelling crimes.)

It is probably best if small children don't answer the door, because they lack the necessary discernment to screen callers. When they are old enough, they should be well-taught three fundamentals:

1. Never open the door without finding out who is there.
2. Never let a caller know they are home alone. Say something such as "My mom can't come to the door right now."
3. Never let people who claim to have an emergency into

the house to use your phone unless they are well-known friends of the family. At most, offer only to make a call for them while they wait outside.

Again, most people who call at your door are harmless, so you don't need to be paranoid—just be prudent.

#19

Lights On

Most burglars and other interlopers, such as Peeping Toms, rely on stealth, so the judicious use of lighting is an important tool in thwarting them. Also, interior lighting helps create the impression that someone is home, which is an effective deterrent to almost all burglars. And some lighting, such as night-lights, increases children's sense of security. So what do you do?

At a minimum, outside lighting should adequately illuminate the entrance habitually used by the family, with all landscaping trimmed so there are no shadows deep enough for someone to lurk within. If you live in a single dwelling, a backyard light is also a good idea. There are now inexpensive timers and dark-sensitive switches that will turn such exterior lights on automatically at dusk.

Also, always leave a light on somewhere in the house at night. This costs only a few cents a month and is excellent insurance against unwelcome intrusions, because would-be offenders have no idea who's home or what's going on, so they will almost certainly pass you by.

Inexpensive heat- and motion-sensitive switches turn a light on automatically when someone enters the room. They are simple to install; just plug them into a socket and plug the light into them. You can also plug a radio or any other appliance into these switches. This is one of the cheapest sorts of alarm and will usually startle intruders into fleeing.

Night-lights placed around the home serve the double purpose of illuminating the house and reassuring children when they get up to go to the bathroom.

#20

Security Alarms

The electronic and computer revolution has been a blessing to personal security. Prices of good security alarms and devices have dropped dramatically in recent years, while quality and reliability have steadily increased. A seemingly endless variety of alarms with combinations of features now exists, with new ones constantly coming on the market, so you'll need to do a bit of research and comparison shopping. Check your electronics store, your chain department store, and the latest edition of *Consumer Reports*, which most libraries carry.

The principle behind security alarms is simple. Some sort of sensor detects an intrusion, which triggers some response—a siren or bell going off, the house lights flashing, an automatic call to a private monitoring company or the local police station, or all of the above. Perimeter alarms are set off when a magnetic contact is broken by someone opening a door or window. Internal space alarms are set off by the motion or body heat of someone entering a room or any protected space where they are set up. Most systems are now wireless, operating on much the same principle as your remote TV tuner, so they are easy to install.

One of the best features of the new systems is the "panic button," which you can carry on your person or keep on your bedside table. You need only push the button to set off the alarm.

If you have active young children and pets paddy-pawing around the house, some alarm setups would be a problem because of all the false alarms triggered. Under these circumstances, the kinds you can set when everyone leaves the house or retires for the night, such as the magnetic perimeter seals on doors and windows, are probably the best.

No alarm will stop highly skilled professionals, but unless you are ostentatiously wealthy or keep state secrets at home, you needn't worry about them—happily you are not worth their time or risk. A home alarm with warning decals prominently displayed is, however, likely to discourage the amateurs and casual intruders. Such an alarm also will shorten the time intruders spend in your dwelling when it is unoccupied. When an alarm goes off, nervous burglars will only snatch whatever is easily accessible, which can cut your losses substantially.

When your children are grown to the point where they and you are regularly gone during most of the day, a centrally monitored alarm system, such as the one by Brinks, can be a good investment. Installation and equipment leasing might cost around $200, with a monthly monitoring fee of under $20. If there is a break-in, the central monitoring station checks it out and calls the police.

Home security systems now usually are produced as components, where you can add additional features as you wish. Smoke alarms and a medical emergency feature can even be tied in, and you can have timers turn various lights and other electrical gear on and off in complicated sequences. Of course, all this elaborate gadgetry is of no protection unless it is *used* correctly and unflaggingly. And your kids will need to learn the ins and outs of it as soon as they're old enough to understand.

How effective are home security alarms? Well, one FBI estimate is that homes with a centrally monitored system are fifteen times less likely to be burglarized successfully. And insurance companies, which give nothing away, are starting to give rate discounts of 5 percent or so for deadbolts and smoke detectors, and up to 20 percent for an alarm system hooked into the police or a central monitoring station.

#21

Children and Telephones

Along with the front door, your telephone is the main contact point between your family and the outside world. It is also an easy means for others to reach in to you and your kids. Because of this, you need to train children in savvy phone use—what to do and not to do.

Without getting paranoid about it, keep in mind that when strangers call, whatever their message, they *are* strangers, and you have no idea what their game is. The following advice is drawn from police crime-prevention units and the federal government's Office of Consumer Affairs.

■ Young children should not answer the telephone until they are old enough and responsible enough to follow phone security guidelines inflexibly. However, they should, as soon as possible, learn to make an emergency call to the police or at least the operator. (Operators historically have been marvelous in giving aid to kids in trouble.) Be sure your child knows your family's name and address.

Children can learn to read numbers early, before they can read words. Some parents make emergency phone cards for their little kids, with big numbers beside drawings of, for instance, you, a cop, the operator, and a neighbor. You can unplug the phone and have them practice dialing and speaking over the phone to summon help.

■ Youngsters (and you) should never give out personal or family information to an unknown person or company over the phone. There's no reason even to give your name; just say

"Hello." It is not a good idea to say "[Smith] residence" or give your phone number, unless this must be done for business reasons.

■ Youngsters should never say they are home alone. If the call is for a parent, they should say something like "She can't come to the phone right now. Can I take a message?"

■ If someone calls and it is a wrong number, teach youngsters not to give out your own name and number. If the caller asks who or what number has been reached, children should ask what number was dialed, then simply say, "You have a wrong number."

■ Youngsters should give no information to phone solicitors. Have them contact the family in writing or call back when an adult is available. Children should *never* give credit card information or information about parents to unknown persons over the phone. They just should insist that the people call back.

■ If youngsters receive an obscene phone call, teach them to just hang up immediately. If an obscene caller persists, don't hesitate to notify the police. Virtually all such characters are harmless, but why chance it?

■ If you use an answering machine, the recommended message for family security is: "Hello, if you leave your name and number, we'll get back to you." Never say "We're not home now." And, unless you need to for business reasons, there is no reason to give your name on the message. Finally, always say "we," because this is discouraging to potential troublemakers.

On the plus side, the telephone is an irreplaceable helpmate in protecting your kids. With it you can reach emergency numbers and hotlines quickly. Through it you also can reach support groups of all kinds. As we'll see, such groups can be very helpful if, for instance, your children get involved with drugs or if family problems affect their security. Having a list of emergency numbers by the phone can be vital. (See the "Where to Get Help" appendix.)

In recent years there has been an explosive growth in toll-free hotlines at the national, state, and local levels. The reason for this growth is simple—such hotlines have proven to be extremely effective in helping people in trouble. These hotlines provide aid and support for a wide range of situations, from rape crisis, to family violence, to suicide prevention, to teenage drug problems, to runaways, to reporting suspected crimes. Surveys have shown that most hotline users are very satisfied with the support and assistance they received.

#22

Mailbox Security

Because criminals are often methodical observers, here are a few security points about your mail.

The best arrangement, if you live in a single dwelling, is a mail slot in or beside your front door that drops the mail inside your house. That way, no one can tell if you are at home, away during the day, or on a trip. A good handyman or mechanically inclined friend can help you install this. If you have an outside mailbox or live in a complex where names are required on the boxes, put two names on the card, one male. If you are a single woman, don't just use your initials; criminals now know all about this trick. You could put the name of a male child alongside yours or just make up a fictitious one. This might give your friends something to gossip about, but two names are far safer than one. You might even put three names on the card.

If you have a mailbox observable from outside your home or complex, it is recommended that you have someone pick up your mail if you will be gone for more than a day or two. An overstuffed mailbox is a clear "nobody home" signal. For the same reason, your kids should empty any externally visible mail in the mailbox on their way home from school.

If you get regular monthly checks, have them deposited directly into your bank account. Any other arrangement is less secure. Consider getting a post office box if you have a small home business with financial transactions or if you routinely get other kinds of sensitive mail that you wouldn't want stolen or read by others.

#23

Getting a Family Dog

A dog can provide increased security plus companionship for the family. In surveys, convicted felons recommend dogs as the second-greatest deterrent, after a security alarm system. Even little dogs make would-be intruders more hesitant, because of the noise they make. A larger dog is a threat of unknown degree to them.

If feasible, it is best to give a dog the run of the house or at least of the areas where intruders might enter. If dogs are locked away, they can't reach intruders.

Veteran security consultant Ira Lipman and other crime experts strongly recommend against having an attack dog. Such dogs need to be highly trained, their trained responses can lapse, and they tend to be unreliable. Also, you are legally liable if your attack dog gets out and attacks someone on its own, which these dogs sometimes do. The intruder they maul can too easily be the mailcarrier or your youngster's playmate. Leave attack dogs to the professionals. You are much better off adopting a friendly pooch from your local animal shelter.

If your child is bitten or threatened by a neighborhood dog, after any needed medical attention, call the police. Owners are legally liable for their dogs. Calling the police will help make the area safer for all inhabitants.

#24

The Gun Gamble

Our nation has had a love affair with guns ever since its colonial beginnings, and the Constitution guarantees all citizens who are not convicted felons the right to bear arms. James Wright, a leading expert on gun issues, says that around half of all American households have at least one firearm. There are some 50 million handguns floating around the country, with 2 million more purchased each year. Private American citizens own far more guns than citizens of most other industrialized nations—and we have far more killings.

Whether or not you have a gun as part of your family's security strategy is a personal and moral decision, but here are some things to consider.

■ There is no question that guns sometimes have been a deterrent to crime in the home—new studies show that what intruders fear most is that some occupant will blow them away. But there also is no question that guns have often been involved in lethal family violence and tragic accidents.

■ Firearms injure and kill far more family members each year than burglars, robbers, or rapists. A recent study by the U.S. Conference of Mayors found that a handgun in the house is far more likely to cause serious injury to a family member than to an intruder.

■ Having a gun without being thoroughly trained in weapons use and safety is about as dangerous as flying an airplane without lessons. Without such training, you are at least as likely to shoot yourself or a bystander as an assailant. And just because you have been trained, remember that your six-year-old child or a visiting acquaintance hasn't. Most children snoop around when the rest of the family is not right there. (Didn't you?)

■ Experts on all sides of the gun issue recommend that guns be locked away and stored unloaded with ammunition locked up separately, whether you have kids or not. Yet an unloaded gun, locked in another room, is likely to do you no good whatsoever during a burglary or robbery.

■ Your children should be told about guns and their dangers as soon as they are old enough to understand, because as they grow up, they may encounter other youngsters who have guns that are *not* toys.

■ Many people who live in rural or isolated wilderness areas own some kind of general-purpose firearm, such as a .22 caliber rifle or pump shotgun. "Trail guns," which are small-caliber, lightweight revolvers, are also popular. Having such a weapon is a good idea, say the experts we consulted, as long as stringent weapon safety guidelines are followed. According to a woman who is raising two youngsters in the northern California forest, a Citizen Band radio with backup battery power is far more useful.

If you move from the city to a rural or wilderness area, check with local authorities and natives about crime safety. They will know the lay of the land.

■ Guns also involve many deep ethical issues. If you do have a firearm and can get to it, do you want to confront an intruder with it? If you're unwilling to actually use it, this will probably telegraph to the interloper. If your own safety or the safety of those you care about is endangered, most people would agree that you are justified in using it. But how about killing someone to prevent them from stealing your VCR? Watching a Western movie is one thing; making an on-the-spot decision about whether to shoot is quite another. Also, in such a confrontation you run the high risk that your opponent is "better with a gun" than you are.

These are some of the facts about firearms, but the ultimate decision is, of course, your own. By following the crimeproofing steps detailed in this book, you and your kids can enjoy vastly increased security from crime without having to become gunslingers.

#25

What to Do About Intruders

What do you do if an unwelcome intruder gets into your dwelling? Crime-prevention experts have developed a few steadfast guidelines that will greatly reduce any risks. These guidelines are based on years of experience and analysis of thousands of cases.

First of all, whatever the circumstances, stay as calm as you can. We know—easier said than done. But the odds are vastly in your favor that you are not dealing with some creature from a Stephen King novel. In almost all cases, the interloper doesn't realize anyone is home. In most of the few remaining cases the offender wants to score some loot quickly and break away with as little hassle as possible.

Sometimes burglars attempt to break into dwellings very quietly to steal. Almost all such intruders are no more interested in confronting you than you are in confronting them. If you awaken and hear someone in your home, start making lots of noise. If you have a personal panic button to set off your home security alarm, push it. Yell something like "Eddie, I hear somebody in the house," whether there's an Eddie with you or not.

If at all possible, you and your kids should not confront the intruder. Criminal intruders will want to flee, so don't block or impede them in any way. If cornered, intruders, who may already be nervous and desperate, often become vicious, like trapped wild animals. Don't try any heroics unless your kids or you are threatened directly. Keep in mind that you and the intruder almost certainly share the same keen interest in getting the whole situation over with as quickly as possible.

On the basis of data from a large number of cases, most crime-prevention experts recommend that if you or your kids awaken to find someone in your room, pretend to be asleep. Again, the odds are that burglars will snatch what they can find and leave.

If a direct confrontation arises and the intruder is armed, there are two choices: Either the intruder will want to escape unhampered, or the situation will become one of armed robbery. If he wants to just flee, let him go with no hassle and no chitchat. If it becomes an armed robbery, give the person what he wants, without arguing or pleading. In his research, veteran criminologist John Conklin found that victims are injured physically most often when they resist a robber.

It is an excellent idea to make your bedroom an inner security center. Your bedroom door should have a good lock, preferably a deadbolt, and when your kids are old enough theirs should too. In an emergency the door can be reinforced by wedging a chair under the handle or using a rubber doorstop. Your bedroom should also have a phone line, if possible. Having an inexpensive battery-operated personal alarm on your nightstand—one that makes lots of noise—is also a good idea. Again, intruders have no idea what an activated alarm might be connected to.

Inexpensive wireless intercoms are on the market with a range of almost a quarter of a mile. With the help of these devices, neighbors are now working out mutual-aid agreements, where they can call each other in case of emergency. The neighbors so notified can then call police and gather together outside, making lots of noise. They too should allow interlopers to flee. Accosting criminals and taking them into custody is strictly police business.

Whatever happens, there are bound to be emotional aftershocks following an intruder incident. In dealing with them, you'll want to accomplish two things. First, let the youngsters talk it out so that any fears are not bottled up, and talk the incident out yourself with a good listener. Second, take preventive measures so the incident doesn't happen again. Then get on with your lives.

#26

Visitors — Friend or Foe

Like most people, you probably regard your dwelling as your private domain, and if you follow the caller guidelines outlined earlier you probably know at least something about anyone who enters. However, your kids are potentially accessible to outside visitors—relatives, baby-sitters, friends—on a regular basis. So it is wise to maintain a degree of guardianship.

For starters, if any visitors are doing something or saying things to your kids that you don't like or approve of, stop them. You can do this politely, but do it firmly, even if they are primary relatives. This is especially true if you are part of a modern "blended family" of ex-spouses, in-laws, stepchildren, and so on. These other people may have views and life-styles that differ markedly from yours, for instance, on sex, drugs, and discipline. So by putting your foot down you may be nipping future trouble in the bud.

If you have an uneasy feeling about some visitor's interactions with your youngsters, curtail the visits and make some other arrangements if you need to see them. Don't just repress such intuitions.

Also, listen to your kids' remarks about visitors. One thing to look for is the difference between mild carping and sullen, stubborn dislike. If the kids are displaying the latter, ask and find out what's up. Nonstrangers are the most frequent source of child abuse and molestation and other mischief.

Good manners are important for your children in getting along with others. Yet even small children should be taught that they have the right to firmly say "No." They should never be taught that they have to go along with the actions of others or be forced to do so for the sake of politeness. If they don't want to kiss Uncle Ben, and if they don't want to play tickle games with the baby-sitter, their feelings should be heeded. There may be no danger at all. But aside from any crime considerations, it *is* their body and their life.

#27

Choosing Baby-sitters

Baby-sitters merit special attention because they have the temporary care and guardianship of your kids in their hands and because they have more than ordinary access to your belongings and personal life. So you need to choose them with care, and establish firm guidelines with them. One mother of two always told sitters, "The kids blab about everything, so I'll know how it went," which she claimed helped keep the sitters reined in.

Special screening and choosing is needed if your child is an infant or toddler, because a young child is more dependent on a sitter than an older one. Also, the tyke won't be able to report what went on to you.

The most common error parents make with baby-sitters is not discussing their own particular ground rules, but just assuming that sitters somehow know them.

You'll want to brief a sitter thoroughly on your family's security practices and perhaps also provide a written copy. This may sound elaborate, but otherwise you may find the sitter innocently opens the door to all callers or tells your children they should always mind grown-ups. If the sitter is a teenager, keep in mind that she doesn't yet have the savvy about the world that you do.

Needless to say, always leave a phone number where you or a reliable adult you know can be reached. The sitter should also be given a list of other emergency numbers.

Most parents we've talked to agree that the best way to find reliable sitters is word of mouth from neighbors and their own personal network. But you still need to check the sitter out yourself and have firm understandings about the house rules. Parents also recommend you not leave tempting small items, such as jewelry, lying around loose; secure them before the sitter comes.

Often there's no problem with the baby-sitter, but there might be with any friends or boyfriends who stop by while one is sitting for you. You'll need to decide whether to allow sitters to have anyone over or not. At the least you'll want any visitors cleared with you. Meet the friend, get his or her name and parent's name and address. The extra visitor might increase security but could also lead to neglect of your kids. Unless you know both the sitter and the friend well, we advise against it.

One thing parents sometimes forget is to not allow the baby-sitter to take the kids anywhere, such as outside to play or out for an ice cream, without parental prior approval.

Always check with your kids afterward on how it went. They might gripe a bit about the sitter not letting them do this or that. But with open communication you can probably easily tell the difference between transient griping and a real situation to dig in to.

Sitters often finish up late at night—a high-risk time—and also might not know your area very well. For these reasons, escort them back to their own home or otherwise see that they get home safely.

#28

Safely Home Alone

At what age does it become okay for your youngsters to be home alone? There's no simple answer to this question.

Your children need to be old enough to follow all the security guidelines, such as not letting strangers in. Also, fire and accident safety have to be taken into account in making the judgment.

If you have more than one child, the older ones also need to be able and willing to be responsible for the security of the younger ones—which really is an additional responsibility.

Ironically, being outside the home on their own, which we discuss in the next chapter, begins to teach children the necessary self-reliance skills for being home alone securely. But you can't just presume that when children reach some arbitrarily specified age they are ready, because kids differ so much in maturity levels. It's also possible that children left alone for long will become lonely or afraid.

Usually a child just sort of grows up to the point where there is mutual parent-youngster agreement that he or she can be left home alone, but this may be dangerously haphazard. It would be better to have short "trial runs" deliberately planned with prior briefings and a check afterward on how the child did. For example, you could start out being gone for a half-hour, while you run an errand. Then you could gradually increase your time away.

Your own job necessities may force you to let your kids be home on their own earlier than you'd like. If possible, arrange for after-school activities, such as library programs, where they have something to do and are near other adults. Here are some cardinal guidelines for when children do need to be home alone for a while.

■ Have them carry the house key on their person, say, inside their clothing. Don't leave a key under the mat or in the flowerpot. Burglars know all about such hiding places and always seem to be able to find them. One habitual burglar said he just watched to see where the kids picked the key up from.

■ Teach children never to let anyone into the house when they're alone without your express permission. This includes other children. *No* exceptions.

■ Also teach them never to tell a caller at the door or on the phone that they are home alone. They should say something like "Mom can't come to the door [phone] right now."

■ If someone tries to force entrance into the house, children should flee to a previously arranged neighbor's house if they can, where the police and you can be called. If they can't get out, they should go to your bedroom-safe room, lock the door, and phone the police, or any prearranged nearby neighbor, and you.

■ Teach them never to accept such statements as "Your mother sent me to get you" from an unknown person. Teach them not to go with anyone you haven't told them specifically to go with, even if they know the person.

■ When children are home alone, it is important for them to make the house appear occupied, for instance, by having lights and a radio on. This will deter virtually all intruders. Daytime burglaries are now more common than night ones, because they are easier and safer for criminals. Tell the children to make enough noise so would-be offenders know someone is home.

■ As a final note, you should realize that when your children are alone they will probably snoop through the house and your things. Most adults we've talked to did so themselves when they were kids. So if you have recreational drugs, guns, intimate letters, and the like, secure them from prying eyes and fingers. Children, like cats, are naturally nosy.

Tactics for handling the "latchkey" situation, where kids are regularly home alone each day, are presented under Strategy 52, "'Latchkey Kid' Security."

#29

A Neighborhood Safety Net

An old Spanish proverb runs: "If you want good service, serve yourself." The residents in more and more neighborhoods are taking this idea to heart and organizing, at least informally, for mutual protection. They are doing this because they are rediscovering something that villagers have known for ages—strangers often won't help each other in emergencies, yet even slight acquaintances usually will.

Even a handful of casual, informal understandings with a few other people living in your area will greatly extend your children's security umbrella. The children will also *feel* more secure and less timid, knowing there are some allies around. And this greater self-confidence will "telegraph" to would-be assailants.

Establishing mutual agreements with other residents in your area is far easier than you might think. The authors have found that neighbors who won't talk with you about other things will usually be more than willing to talk over and do something about crime security, because virtually everyone now has some concern about it.

A lot of research demonstrates how effective such neighborhood networking can be. For instance, the National Crime Prevention Council reports that *Neighborhood Watch programs have cut crime rates to less than half of what they were in some communities.* On a recent national television program, one veteran burglar sneered at Neighborhood Watch arrangements, yet further questioning revealed that reports to the police from suspicious neighbors had led to his own arrest and conviction.

Be sure your youngsters are introduced to the other network

people so that they easily recognize each other. And get to know who the other kids in your immediate area are. No one has to become fast friends—just recognized acquaintances with a shared desire to deter crime. Even if you dislike a neighbor, back him or her up in security measures. You and your neighbors can make protection from crime part of your daily life, just by watching out for each other. The mere presence of others will halt most crimes in progress because criminals shun publicity.

Most police departments are more than happy to help a neighborhood or dwelling complex set up a crime-watch program. Four out of five law enforcement units in the United States now have some sort of crime-prevention unit. Such units significantly reduce crime. For information, call police at their workday business number, not the 911 emergency line. Aside from helping organize and supplying start-up data, the police will usually provide a continuing liaison to help with any crime problems that develop. These units also usually provide free home security inspections and make recommendations for increasing your protection. Even in high-crime areas, there is documented evidence that such grass-roots organizations have taken neighborhoods back from criminal elements.

These organizations are sometimes very effective in mounting concerted action to get a local school to curtail drug trafficking or local officials to institute crime-protection measures, such as better street lighting. Even two or three complaining people have far more weight than one.

Some neighborhood groups establish designated "safe houses" where children always can go in case of trouble.

If you live in a housing complex, attend tenant association meetings and bring up security issues. We can virtually guarantee you'll find receptive ears.

Maybe you are a loner and not inclined to get involved. But at the very least, strike some agreements with a couple of nearby neighbors. Your children's safety may depend on it.

#30

Tell the Police

You might have mixed feelings about the police. You don't want them to give you a speeding ticket, and maybe you were distressed by some scandal involving individual officers or departments somewhere in the country. But if there's trouble, a police officer or security person is likely to be your children's best friend. Police officers have a longstanding tradition of protecting and helping children, and their overall record in this area is outstanding. The police are a vital part of your children's security umbrella.

All crime experts agree on the importance of teaching children early that police (and private security personnel) are friends who can help them. In later years they may wish to hide some of their illicit doings from the cops, but they still should be able to turn to them if they run into real trouble.

Report crimes against your home and family to the police. According to Department of Justice Victimization Survey studies, less than half the crimes against persons and only one-fourth of property crimes are ever reported to the police. This gross underreporting only makes life more secure for the *criminals*.

Sometimes people are wary of any contact with the police because of petty crimes they themselves have committed. However, in virtually all instances, the police aren't interested. Their concern is the real troublemakers. So you and they share a deep interest in keeping the peace and having the world be a safer place for families.

Don't threaten to call the police; just do it.

Sometimes people feel it isn't worth the trouble to report a crime because it's no use; nothing will happen to the perpetrator anyway. It is true that the culprit might not be indicted for the crime being reported. The chance that a criminal will be convicted for any single crime is discouragingly low; but the chance that he or she will be convicted eventually is almost certain. The more often crimes are reported and the more police data that accumulate, the sooner such apprehension and imprisonment will occur.

Report suspicious incidents or suspected crimes in your neighborhood to the police. There is an excellent "self-interest" reason for doing so. Crime has a tendency to spread and spill over in a locale, like a spilled drink on a table. You can do the reporting anonymously if you wish. Just give as many details as you can, descriptions, license numbers, addresses—no detail is too trivial. "Trivial" items often supply the missing piece. Around 95 percent of all the information authorities have to work with comes from private citizens. By such reporting, you will help make your home and the area you live in safer for all the kids around.

#31

Dealing with Domestic Violence

Most people envision their home as their sanctuary from the wider world. The ideal is that the home will be the setting for a harmonious and fulfilling family life.

This is a dream, never entirely achieved by real-life families. No family is entirely free from tensions, disputes, disappointments, and temporary falling-outs among the members. Brothers and sisters pound one another, parents sometimes vacillate between being too neglectful and being too harsh; and few spouses are able to practice "love me tender" all the time. Yet there is usually enough affection and good times to carry things along. But if things get to the point where there is real physical, emotional, or sexual abuse going on, the family is in trouble.

Family violence is a complicated psychological and legal subject, but there is a bottom line: *If you are involved in a family violence situation, do something about it.*

Don't just go on hoping it will all turn out well, as in a romance novel. Research clearly shows that if abuse has happened before, it is very likely to happen again, unless you or others strongly intervene. Without such intervention, abuse usually becomes habitual.

If you are in such a dysfunctional situation you may feel trapped and helpless, living with the dark merry-go-round of violence, reconciliation, growing tension, violence, and so on. Or you may discover sexual abuse within the family. Such vicious circles seldom stop by themselves. But you can begin to take some steps.

For starters, talk to someone about it. There are now hotlines, women's centers, and child abuse centers where you can discuss your situation over the phone anonymously. By talking over the problem, you can become more clear-headed about your situation and start looking at your options. Just telling somebody who's a good listener begins to ease the anguish and get a load off your shoulders. (The number for the National Coalition Against Domestic Violence hotline is 1 800 333–SAFE.)

As an abused person, you are going through the equivalent of a serious illness, and you need outside help. You need to "*Go Public*" (*Mega-Strategy Four*) with your situation for everyone's sake. You should tell as many organizations, friends, and relatives as possible. The abuse usually happens and continues in isolation. By going public, you are psychologically and legally less powerless in the relationship. Abusers often have little sense that they are doing anything wrong, and it can take strong "reality intervention" by the police, or even a marital separation, to wake them up. In *Men Against Women*, veteran abuse researcher Edward Gondolf points out: "The best way to help a violent man is to convince him that violence won't be tolerated."

Don't just go along with an abysmal situation for the sake of the kids. A violent home scene cannot be a safe or happy place for anyone. People thrive in nurturant, cooperative surroundings, but they wilt in the face of chronic discord. Also, there is a well-documented tendency for children who are abused or who witness parental violence to grow up to be abusive parents and spouses.

But have heart and hope, because hundreds of thousands of cases show that it is never too late to better a bad family situation if you just begin to act on it.

If you realize that you are an abuser, three things have proven most helpful. First, recognize that you really have a serious problem. Second, communicate with support groups such as RAVEN or Parents Anonymous, or a counselor, or at least a friend. (See the "Where to Get Help" appendix.) Support groups are having excellent results in helping people break out of these devastating situations. Third, read up on the subject of family violence and child abuse so that you become more knowledgeable and aware. The consequences of not changing are simply grim.

If you were an abused child, work to heal the wounds so that you don't pass it on to the next generation.

If you are a relative, neighbor, or friend of a family where there is child abuse or violence, don't shut your eyes to it. Very seldom do such abusive patterns clear up by themselves, and the participants do not outgrow them. However, you have to use some real judgment in this—many parents spank their small children, have some marital spats, and hug their kids without being abusive, and many families do things differently than you would. Real abuse and violence go far beyond these things. If you know the abuser or abused person, you can be a friend. Let him or her open up to you about it, and steer the person toward help. If the patterns persist, report it to your local welfare agency or the police. You can report it anonymously if you need to. A good first step would be to talk the situation over with someone at your local women's center.

#32

Moving to a New Place

It is becoming very common for a family to live in several places while children are growing up. Each new place calls for a full reassessment of the children's security from crime. The main point is that neither you nor the kids can presume that things are the same in the new place as they were in your last location. They might be better in some respects, worse in others, but they are bound to be *different* in some important ways. The kids also may be more vulnerable during the transition, so it is important to "*Keep in Touch*" (*Mega-Strategy One*) with them.

You have new neighbors, new delivery schedules, a dwelling with new entryways, new streets and stores, and new life-styles going on around the home. All this deserves a fresh "*Check It Out*" (*Mega-Strategy Six*).

Ask questions. Talk to other grown-ups and kids in the area about risks and opportunities. Chat with store clerks, your new neighbors, the local cops, and delivery people about "how it is around here." Ask what you and your youngsters should look out for. Explore the area together with your kids. Work at getting acquainted.

A new place *is* a new place. Both you and your youngsters are temporarily innocent of the scene—who's who and what's what. Be a little extra cautious and alert until the family has learned the new ropes.

4

Going Out Safely with Kids

From the time your children are born until the time they finally leave the nest, there will be an almost endless parade of occasions when you take them on forays outside your home. By following some guidelines, these treks can be made far more secure for both the kids and you.

Taking your kids out for chores or pleasure also gives you many chances to teach them how to avoid crime out in the wider world. You can train them by your own example, by giving them some direct hands-on experience, and by verbal explanations. Even toddlers will begin to copy how you handle situations—what you say and do. They will then be much more certain about what to do when they go out on their own.

#33

Staying Together and Staying Public

Two people out together are far more than twice as safe as one alone, even when one of them is a child. Whether alone or together, anyone at any age is also far safer staying in public view and keeping to populated areas. These two facts cannot be said too often, and they have dozens of specific applications.

For instance, going out together means *staying* together, in the parking lot, in elevators, and in the restrooms when the kids are small. Even when you are out together, stay in public view. Avoid isolated spots, back stairways, deserted areas, and secluded shortcuts. Reports from convicted felons show that they look for loners and usually pass by two or more people, even when one is a youngster, because it's too much possible hassle. And they look for loners in isolated circumstances.

Avoid the for-a-moment habit because it increases risks. Don't leave your child alone while you dash back in to ask something of a clerk, or send your kid back in to pick up a receipt while you wait. Don't leave the kids in the car while you run in for a few items at the grocery store. Continue to stay together.

If you must leave the children for a bit, leave them in a populated place, ideally under the watchful eye of a store security officer or receptionist. And have the firm understanding that they won't stray. By the teenage years, children are much less at risk, but the two of you are still better off sticking together. Most kids like to run around, so you'll need to take this into account, and maybe rein them in with some discipline.

Staying together and in public view is especially important

if you are going into downtown urban areas, which nowadays are so often an odd combination of posh professional suites and sleazy street crime. Wherever you are, if you encounter anything suspicious, don't hesitate to find a security person or at least a clerk. If you are handling sums of money or any expensive purchases, ask to be accompanied safely to your car by security. And don't even go into such areas with your kids at night if you can at all help it. If you grocery shop with children, having the bag attendant help you to your vehicle provides added security.

Work out in advance what children should do if they become separated from you. There are two basic options: The first is to agree that the children will go to some easily spotted landmark, such as a central courtyard or the lobby of a professional building. The second is to teach the children to contact a security guard or clerk and say that you've been separated. Keep in mind that it is easy for young children (or even adults sometimes) to lose their bearings in a large shopping mall or building. Both authors have themselves gotten lost temporarily in such structures. Just because you can easily find "the bench by the fountain," for instance, in a mall you've been to several times, don't assume your six-year-old can too. It's not a bad idea to have a "practice run" with your children; have them lead you to the agreed-upon place to be sure they know the way.

The combination of staying together and staying public effectively thwarts almost all types of crime.

#34

Car Security

Chauffeuring kids around seems to be a routine part of most parents' lives. A few inflexible habits can make all the difference in the children's protection during these treks.

An obvious point is to keep your "taxi" vehicle in good running order—adequate tires and brakes, enough gas and oil, tuneups, checkups, and so on. Aside from accident safety and convenience, all passengers and the driver will be more secure crimewise if your vehicle is dependable. Select your car with dependability in mind.

"Close and Lock" (*Mega-Strategy Three*). Lock *all* vehicle doors and keep all windows closed, even when you are in a familiar or supposedly safe place. To speak with someone, or for ventilation, roll windows down at most an inch or so. Do these things when you are in the car and also when you leave the car, even for a minute. These points might seem obvious. Yet Department of Justice surveys show that over half the car thefts and break-ins result from unlocked doors and windows. In an estimated 20 percent of car thefts, the keys had been left in the ignition.

Always park in a well-populated location, as near to where you're going as possible. At night you'll also want it to be well lighted. After you park, look around your immediate surroundings before you and your kids get out. If you sense anything suspicious, start the car and park somewhere else. While returning to the car, again, look over the immediate area. If *anything* seems suspicious, such as loiterers or a vehicle blocking your exit, turn around and go get some help. Most public areas now have security personnel on duty who can aid you.

When returning to the car, always glance inside it before getting in, to be sure no one is hiding there. If the car looks as if it has been broken into, go get help.

Going to and from your vehicle are usually the times of greatest exposure, so stay alert for anything out of the ordinary.

Whenever you go out with your kids (or alone), these tips should become automatic ingrained habits. Don't become complacent and let them slip because "nothing ever happens." The probable reason that "nothing ever happens" is *because* of such habits.

Be especially alert when driving through high-crime districts. Double-check that *all* doors and windows are locked, and don't leave the security of your car if anything at all suspicious happens. Criminals will sometimes run up at a stoplight and jump into your car if the passenger door or back doors are unlocked. Don't converse with strangers in such areas. If you must do so, roll thc window down only an inch or two. Scc that the kids know these rules well. The same rules will still apply when they've grown up and are driving.

Never leave your children alone in the car, even for a "back in a minute," if you can possibly help it. When you keep them with you, you are both safer. If you must leave them in the car, see that the doors and windows are secured and you have the keys. If the weather is hot, roll windows down only a bit for ventilation. And train them not to interact with strangers while you're away. Teach them to lean on the horn if there's trouble.

If you are dropping the children off somewhere, chaperone them in to where they're going, or at least stay put long enough to see that they get inside safely. Do this also when you are ferrying other people's kids or your baby-sitter.

While driving, don't pick up hitchhikers or anyone you don't know well. If you come upon someone having car trouble or some other mishap, don't get out of your car. Offer to call the police or an auto club, but don't unlock your door or roll your window down more than a couple of inches. Such staged incidents are now a frequent road practice of perpetrators with robbery or other unpleasantries in mind.

While you are on the road, don't be argumentative with other drivers. *"Get Along"* (*Mega-Strategy Seven*). Drive in such a way as to put distance between you and any obviously irate or intoxicated motorist or anyone tailgating you.

Should you purchase a car alarm and other security devices? Yes, but you need to check out the range of alternative items at your auto parts store, comparison shop, and select the system that fits your needs and your budget. No system will thwart the sophisticated, determined pro, but any system may deter the amateurs and semipros so that they go elsewhere, especially when you also display the warning decals.

Basic workable systems cost around $150, and the stores that sell them usually install them for a reasonable fee. If you can't afford a system, you can buy a "decoy" LED alarm indicator for around $20 that will make would-be perpetrators think your car is effectively secured.

The most common alarm unit includes a circuitry sensor (which triggers if doors, trunk, or hood are opened), a motion sensor (which picks up on glass breakage or tampering), and a remote transmitter (for arming and disarming). The remote keychain control also can be used as a panic button to set off the alarm if you run into trouble while your family is on the way to and from the car. Additional features, such as a starter disabler and steering wheel lock, can be added for a few dollars more. Some insurance companies now offer discounts if you install a car alarm system.

When you and your kids arrive back home again, take a moment to see that everything looks okay before getting out of the car. If there are signs of a break-in, do not, repeat, *do not* enter your dwelling. Go to a neighbor or a nearby phone and call the police. You want to avoid a possible confrontation with any intruder. Keep the children close by you until the situation is cleared up.

#35

What to Do If Stranded

What do you do if you're out with your kids and have car trouble or are otherwise stranded? The following street-wise recommendations from the highway patrol and auto clubs explain how safely to handle being stranded.

What to do depends on the circumstances, but there are two guidelines to adhere to, whatever the situation: First, stay close and together with your youngsters; don't become separated. Second, don't accept help offered by unknown persons who are not the authorities, beyond having them call for assistance for you. If they have a car phone or CB radio, this is easy for them to do. Kids often become whiny under adverse conditions, but don't give in, for instance, and let them stay in the car by themselves.

If you discover you are stranded, take a few deep breaths to calm yourself, assess your situation, and look at your resources and options.

If you have just left some establishment and your car won't start, your best bet is to go back inside to phone for assistance. Be wary of anyone who suddenly appears and offers to help you get the car started. Robbers who may have disabled the car deliberately sometimes use this tactic.

If you are in unknown surroundings you may feel anxious and uncertain, but any gas station, convenience store, or commercial building can serve as a haven. Assess the area around you. Also reassure the kids that everything will be okay.

If it is night and there is nothing open nearby, use your car as your sanctuary, camping inside if necessary until daylight. If you have a personal car alarm, you can trigger it until someone becomes annoyed enough to call the police. You could also lean on your horn. Focus on security, not comfort. If your car is still running, but you have a flat tire or mechanical difficulty, drive carefully to a populated area or main thoroughfare. There may be damage, but security comes first.

If you are on the open road with kids and have car trouble, immediately switch on your hazard lights and get over to the shoulder and out of traffic. Again, treat your car as your sanctuary. Raise your hood and tie a white cloth to the top of it, which is now a widely recognized distress signal. You can also get, or make, a cardboard "Please Call Highway Patrol" sign to put in your back window. If someone stops, only ask the person to call the highway patrol, your auto club, or a relative. Don't accept other help from passersby because robbers now sometimes cruise the highways looking for stalled motorists. Stay in the car; a highway patrol officer or police officer is likely to stop by soon and help you. If you do have to leave the car, secure it, then all leave together.

Whenever you need to stop temporarily, find a well-lighted, well-peopled area. And finally, be sure you have enough gas and oil at all times. Never "bet you'll probably make it" to the nearest gas station. Being stranded out of gas in an unknown area, at night, or miles from the nearest service station is both dangerous and horrendously inconvenient.

Even well-maintained vehicles can suffer breakdowns, so making some contingency preparations is advisable, especially if you travel regularly with your children. Experts recommend assembling a "breakdown kit" containing essential tools, flares, a first-aid kit, flashlight, a sealed tin of cookies, and a sealed bottle of liquid. It is an excellent idea to join an auto club and always carry its emergency number, as well as numbers you might need.

The cost of car phones and their monthly charges continue to drop, so you might consider getting one for security, if you can afford it. With a car phone you have the police, cab companies, your auto club, and your support network immediately available.

#36

Restroom Safety

Needing to use the bathroom is an inevitable part of going out with kids. Isolated restrooms in parks, beaches, deserted sections of malls, professional buildings, or quiet libraries especially deserve to be used with caution.

As usual, you have a double agenda:

1. Ensure the immediate security of the children.
2. Train them in effective restroom security tactics.

When children are small, just take them into the restroom with you even if they are of the "opposite" sex.

When children are older you can stand outside the door, perhaps saying loudly, "I'll be right outside," so that anyone in the bathroom will hear you. If you become suspicious, go right in—don't stand on ceremony. By the time they are adolescents your youngsters will be able to go by themselves, and they will also be on their own a great deal. Long before that time, they should have learned restroom security.

- Teach kids to mind their own business in a public restroom. They shouldn't loiter, engage in chatter with other occupants, respond to other's remarks, or make comments about anyone else, even if they are with a companion.
- If they sense anything odd, out of the ordinary, or suspicious, they should turn around and leave immediately. Better to risk wetting their pants than walk into a bad scene.

- If possible, children always should go into a restroom when there is a good flow of traffic in and out.
- Teach them not to place purses, packages, or other belongings in such a way that they can be grabbed easily by a snatch-and-run artist. If they use a stall, they should place items back from the entrance and keep a grip and an eye on them.

Most public restrooms are safe. Even if a child is propositioned, a firm no almost always handles it. Following the preceding tips will virtually eliminate any risks.

#37

On the Spot: Dealing with Robbery

Veteran crime researcher John Conklin did extensive interviews with ninety robbery victims in the Boston area. They reported that they had been selected by the robbers because they were alone, appeared to have money, and were in an isolated location. Convicted muggers report choosing their prey for these very reasons.

These findings provide strong leads for avoiding robbery when out with your kids. Don't be alone; don't flash money or valuables; and don't go into isolated areas.

But muggings and store holdups still happen sometimes, even in public places and when there are several people together. And as they grow up, your children are even more likely to encounter "petty" robbery of their lunch money, bus passes, and so on. So what do you and they do if confronted by an actual robbery situation?

The most important thing to know about robbers is this: *In virtually all cases, muggers are interested only in getting your money or valuables and getting away as quickly as possible*. Anything that slows them down makes them more nervous and therefore more dangerous. They have no interest in sob stories or arguments, and they are usually prepared to meet force with force, if necessary.

So give them what they want immediately, with no idle chatter. If your child starts to say something, tell him or her sternly to be quiet. Controlling your own child will reassure the robber that you're not going to give him any trouble. You and the mugger have a shared goal of getting the incident over with as quickly as possible, so do nothing to jeopardize this goal.

From his extensive studies, Conklin concluded that victims who believed they could overpower their assailants and resisted were the most likely to be injured. A woman alone has some chance of being raped as well as robbed, so resistance should be considered as an option. However, with kids along, rape is extremely unlikely. As mentioned, virtually all muggers want to get away as quickly as they can. You want exactly the same thing, so cooperate.

If you and your kids are present during a store holdup, quickly do what the robbers say. Realize that you may be dealing with unstable people. Make no unnecessary moves and say nothing unnecessary. Don't try to be a hero; you are not faster than a speeding bullet. Virtually anything that you do, aside from complying, increases the likelihood that someone will get hurt.

You can greatly reduce your likelihood of being mugged by the judicious handling of money and valuables. There's usually no reason to wear gold chains and expensive watches, for instance. And take extra care with any money transactions. Don't use an automatic teller machine in an isolated spot or during off hours. If you have a large money transaction at the bank or are making expensive purchases, feel free to ask security or an employee to see you safely to your car. If you have an uneasy feeling, act on it.

Finally, all crime experts make this most basic recommendation: "Don't take along more cash than you can afford to lose."

#38

Surviving Street Violence

Crime actually never happens randomly, but it might seem so if you and your children are out, minding your own business, and violence erupts around you. Happily, this is rare in most locales. But it *does* happen. Even in such a situation, however, you are far from helpless, and your own actions can make all the difference.

If you see people acting violently or irrationally, do what you can to get yourself and your youngsters away from the scene. If you are walking, go into a building, go the other way, or cross the street. Forget about curiosity; security for you and yours is the priority.

When you are driving with children (or by yourself), never try to pass people driving erratically. Don't presume they are rational or under self-control. Consider getting their license number and reporting them to the police, at least anonymously. But don't play games with them. If they insult you, stay cool and keep your own temper. Remember, you may be dealing with psychotics or people under the influence of who knows what.

If you are driving through town and encounter a violent street scene, *immediately* check to see that all car doors are locked and get away from the area.

If you are on foot and gunfire erupts, getting twenty feet away makes you and your youngsters more than twice as safe as ten feet away. And a hundred feet away is many, many times safer. Even if the person is shooting directly at you, every few more feet of distance away will greatly reduce your likelihood of being hit, as any marksman can attest. Luckily, most criminals are not good marksmen. It takes much training and practice to fire either a handgun or an automatic weapon accurately.

After you've moved away, or if you can't move away, drop to the ground. For instance, if you see or hear a police-versus-criminals gun battle, or a crazy shooting spree, immediately drop to the ground and train your children to do the same. Depending somewhat on distances and type of weapons, this cuts the odds of being hit to one-tenth or less of what they would be if you remain standing or sitting. Drop to the floor even if you are inside a building, because modern high-powered weapons have tremendous penetrating power.

If you are home and hear gunfire outside, don't peer out your windows to see what's going on. Have everyone drop to the floor and stay there. Stay very low if you move around—crawling is best. Check that your doors are locked and then call the police. Don't let curious children peer out. Get everyone away from the side of the house nearest the gunfire. It it gets quiet outside, don't presume everything is all over—there just may be a lull in the battle.

Throughout history, getting away and dropping to the ground have saved millions of lives, even in the midst of raging battles, and they can serve you and your children as well.

■ If you encounter street violence, move away as best you can.

■ After moving away, or if you can't get away, immediately drop to the ground.

■ Curb any curiosity and get yourself and your kids to cover.

■ If you are driving and run into street violence or erratic motorists, immediately check that all car doors are locked and drive a safe distance away or let the erratic motorists get way ahead of you. Pull off into a public place if you're being followed.

■ If you are home and hear gunfire or outside commotion, get the family to drop immediately to the floor, stay low, check that doors are locked, and forbid any curious peeking by children.

■ Don't attempt to be a hero. Your job is to see to the safety of your family.

#39

Professional Services and Disservices

As your children grow from birth to young adulthood, there will be times when they need professional services of one kind or another. And you probably will have to do most of the deciding on which professionals and what services. So how do you find a good doctor, dentist, day-care center, child counselor, or investment advisor for your child, who will serve your needs well and not take advantage of the fact that you are no expert in the area yourself?

"Check It Out" (*Mega-Strategy Six*) is the watchword. There are fads (and frauds) in pediatrics, orthodontics, child care, elective surgeries, college investment funds, and child development theories.

Children can be vulnerable to more than just street violence. Experts make their living advising and carrying out treatments of all sorts for kids, and parents often are not well enough informed to question their recommendations. Remember, professional assessments often have an entrenched bias, reflecting the preconceptions of the professional's field of expertise. It should be no big surprise that surgeons tend to recommend surgery, orthodontists tend to recommend braces, counselors tend to recommend counseling, and stock brokers tend to recommend a college-fund stock portfolio.

You might feel a bit helpless when it comes to technical decisions about your kids, yet there are things you can do to increase the likelihood that you'll get service, not disservice.

■ Unless it is an emergency and you have no choice, never just select a professional cold out of the yellow pages. Ask your neighbors and others in your network who have children for recommendations and query them about their experiences. This tactic is not 100 percent reliable and won't necessarily get the best person, but it will probably save you from the worst. Every field, from medicine to music and dance instructors to youth counselors to evangelists, has its share of incompetents and shady characters, who nevertheless remain in practice. Ask professionals in any field. If they are candid, they'll admit that they know of colleagues who shouldn't be allowed to practice. Difficulties in getting evidence, fear of lawsuits, and reluctance to "show dirty laundry in public" all lessen the chances of anything being done about them, except in the most flagrant cases. Word-of-mouth referrals are a strong safeguard against such practitioners.

■ Keep in mind that professionals (including public officials) are supposed to be working for *you.* Professionals sometimes develop an arrogant viewpoint that you and your kids are their wards; that they know best and you shouldn't be disobedient to their decisions and advice. They *may* be giving good advice and direction, but they are very far from always right.

■ Be wary of any professional who discourages you from asking questions. Part of any expert's job should be explaining the situation to you until you understand your options. Keep in mind that a professional's assessments are only judgment calls, not Immutable Truths. Never just presume some experts knows best.

■ Unless you are faced with an emergency, investigate the subject as thoroughly as you can. The more you know, the more you are able to ask intelligent questions and make your own independent decisions. Reference librarians at your local library can be wonderfully helpful in doing this. Whether the recommendation is for elective surgery, a special child-care program, an eating disorder treatment, drug rehabilitation, or a college fund, try to get a variety of opinions and knowledge sources. For instance, most government and private insurance programs strongly encourage getting second opinions about any nonemergency surgery. The U.S. Department of Health and Human Services points out: "Second opinions are your right as a patient," and "Many conditions may be treated just as effectively without surgery."

And don't just get a second opinion from the person down the hall who went to the same school, because this is likely to be just an echo, not an alternative. For example, you might check with a certified holistic health center or nutritionist as well as the traditional medical approach to some condition. Do the best you can.

■ If your early contact with the professional makes you feel uneasy, listen to your intuitions and go elsewhere.

■ Keep in close communication with your youngsters all through their experiences with any professional. Most practitioners are sincere and competent, yet even some famous ones have not been above molestation or other abuses.

Using these guidelines will help you avoid not only criminal fraud but also incompetence and expensive unnecessary treatment of your kids at the hands of professionals of every kind.

#40

Family Trips

Travel brings the excitement of new activities and situations, but also new potential risks for children. Those risks can, however, be minimized with a few precautions.

First off, for the whole family's peace of mind, take steps to secure your dwelling while you are away. The number-one tactic is to set things up so the home appears occupied. Use timers to turn on lights, radio, and TV in different parts of the house at different times of the day and night. And have a friend or neighbor pick up newspapers, mail, and other deliveries off your exterior grounds. If you can afford it, a reliable house sitter is a good move. Needless to say, as you are leaving, check to see that all entries and windows are closed and locked securely.

All the time you and the youngsters are on your trip, keep the seven mega-strategies in mind and apply them to the new situations you encounter. You want these strategies to become habitual. All the specific pointers made earlier about going out safely apply double, because you're going into unknown territory. Even nearby regions may have slightly different customs and different ways of doing things.

The two main crime-avoidance concerns while traveling are thievery of one sort or another and risks to kids stemming from unfamiliar places and situations.

When traveling, use credit cards and insured travelers' checks. Carry only a modest amount of cash, and don't put all your cash in one place on your person. Use inexpensive luggage that is not inviting. If you fly or use other public transport, claim your luggage immediately. Airport thieves look for luggage that goes around the carousels more than a couple of times. If you are driving, have a good map and your route worked out so you don't end up wandering around, off the beaten path.

Most hotels and motels are fairly secure as long as the members of your family use common sense. The management is eager to avoid incidents, so personnel can be counted on almost always to help in case of trouble. However, stay out of back sections or dimly lit isolated areas in the building and grounds. And ask about safety in the immediate area; don't assume security is handled for you.

Without being paranoid about it, approach elevators and hallways alertly. If anything makes you feel uneasy, go back to the desk and ask to be escorted to your room. Report anything suspicious to security or the management. The whole family also should be prudent when interacting with strangers.

And don't just presume the hotel has supplied all the room security you need. Do your own check. Doors usually have a lock, deadbolt, and chain—use them all. But check out any balcony doors and the bathroom windows, because these are the most common intruder entries. Don't leave valuables lying around in your room. The hotel safe is a better place for them.

When visiting relatives or friends in another locale, your family should keep up its own security habits. Get the kids to understand that they are not on their own home turf so they don't know the lay of the land or "the way things are done" where you are visiting. For instance, they may innocently think that because a playground or swimming pool is safe in their home area, that it's also safe where they're visiting—which might or might not be true. Consult with those who are living there.

There's no need to be overanxious about family trips; millions of people travel safely all the time. Just don't be foolish, careless, or negligent. Traveling, like life, is always something of a venture, where, to a large extent, you make your own odds.

#41

Foreign Travel Security

In a recent travel advisory, the U.S. State Department stated that crime against travelers is a growing problem worldwide, especially in the big cities. No country can provide absolute protection to visitors, so travelers need to watch out for themselves.

The State Department and a veteran travel agent offer a few special security tips if you travel abroad with your kids.

Do some checking on any place you are thinking about visiting. As the news headlines have demonstrated during these last few years, the world is now a volatile place and you don't want to walk innocently into a major civil upheaval. Most industrialized countries are safe; in fact, many are far safer than the streets of our own nation. Third World and developing countries are another matter. If you are planning a trip to one of these, do some extra homework beforehand. Use the *Reader's Guide to Periodical Literature* at your local library to find some recent magazine articles on the country, and see what's currently going on there. Get a couple of up-to-date guidebooks, check with experienced travel agents and, if possible, with people who have been there recently. Dig beneath the beautiful travel brochures to get more of the real story of current conditions there. Ask your travel agent if there are any State Department travel advisories on the country you're considering. Or you can call the State Department's Citizen's Emergency Center at 202 647–5225, but don't rely *only* on these government advisories. Per *Mega-Strategy Six*, "*Check It Out.*"

Chances are, you will be recognized as a foreigner by the

natives of the country you're visiting. Tourism is a major industry for many countries, so they bend over backward to attract and accommodate tourists. Yet as a tourist, you are also a prime target for petty (and not so petty) robberies, fraud, and hit-and-run crimes. And there are criminals everywhere in the world. This calls for some extra precautions. Stay away from black markets. Deal only with authorized outlets when you exchange money or buy tickets. It is a good idea to travel in groups and don't go far off the beaten path and into out-of-the-way areas unless you are experienced. Also apply all the recommendations in "Family Trips" (Strategy 40). Guard your belongings with special care at airports, train terminals, and on the streets. In every place in the world, there are safe and dangerous areas; find out, and if in doubt, don't risk the questionable places.

In many countries you may be especially vulnerable to swift-footed pickpockets, purse-snatchers, camera grabbers, and such—and often they will be young children. You are also a prime target for fraudulent local "bargain" merchandise. Kidnapping is also not unknown, so the tactic of staying close to your kids (Strategy 33) goes double in a foreign land.

While many travelers don't realize it, your family should keep in mind this very important point: *While in a foreign country, you are subject to* its *laws*. Unless you are a government official, you have no diplomatic immunity and your country's consulate can do surprisingly little for you if you get into legal trouble. For instance, drunken driving charges may be unbelievably grim. Older children especially should know not to buy illicit drugs or engage in other illegal behavior. Despite all the stories about exotic foreign romances, they also need to be very cautious about any sexual involvements. Any clout you may have in protecting them back home probably means *nothing* in the place you are visiting.

When you go to a different country, realize that you are

plunging into a different *culture*, whose ways may differ markedly from your family's. For instance, in some countries women still can't vote or drive cars and children are expected to remain quiet whenever an adult is present. Your fashion magazine, picked up at the airport, may also be regarded as pornography by the locals. So enjoy yourselves but be respectful of local ways.

5

Out on Their Own

As your children grow they come into ever-widening contact with the world outside your home. They progress from home to yard to neighborhood to school to all over town and beyond. As they do so, they encounter new experiences and broader horizons. They also encounter new potential hazards.

Kids going out on their own really are innocent about the wider world. It is a mistake to assume otherwise. Parents have to strike a tricky, ever-shifting balance between allowing freedoms and imposing constraints. Children want to explore the world. Parents want to protect them from its pitfalls.

As your youngsters grow, there will be more and more times when you won't be with them—but your influence will. This chapter takes up the common situations as kids begin to "move outside," such as traveling to and from school, screening strangers, getting help, maintaining bicycle security, preventing molestation, and being "latchkey kids." The entries outline ways of teaching and applying the seven mega-strategies so that your guardianship remains effective when they go out on their own.

#42

Help Me!

Knowing how to get help is a basic human survival skill. A child needs to be taught how to get help, from the earliest age onward. This is vital not only in avoiding crime but also for getting assistance in case of fire, injuries, or natural disasters. The ability to find aid needs to go far beyond just yelling "Mommy!"

Help is actually widely available to kids, but they must learn how to get it. *Children have to be taught how to get help*, just as they have to be taught the alphabet. And, like learning the alphabet, there has to be repetition and practice. If they become scared or confused, children can easily forget haphazard instructions; this is why some drilling is so important. Adults regularly fail to realize just how unacquainted with the outside world children really are. For instance, we spoke with one child who had the mistaken notion that the police somehow just automatically came to save you if there was trouble (an idea probably picked up from television).

Specific tips for getting help are scattered throughout the pages of this book, because getting help is the answer in so many types of potential crime situations. The possibility that help might arrive is also the greatest deterrent to most crimes in progress. For instance, an adult's arrival on the scene usually will stop an in-progress bullying or mugging of a child by other kids.

The fundamental lesson for your youngsters to learn is that there is plenty of help out there, but in most cases it is not automatic—they have to reach for it. Training turns raw recruits into soldiers and amateur plunkers into musicians, and it will turn little kids into survivors.

■ Teach children that any public place, such as a store, a library, a fire station, or an office, can be used as a sanctuary if they are in trouble. As long as there are grown-ups around, they are almost certainly safe. They should tell an adult what's going on and ask for help.

■ Any utility truck, repair truck, cab, garbage truck, or work crew can be approached as a likely source of help. Most of these are now radio linked to a central office and dispatchers who can help in an emergency if asked. (Trucks displaying the Officer McGruff dog-in-a-trench-coat sign are part of the National Crime Prevention network and have pledged to aid any kid in trouble.)

■ If children feel threatened, are being followed or hassled, they can ask any teacher, crossing guard, uniformed person, or another grown-up for help. Teach them to persist—if the first person fails to help, a second or third almost certainly will. Also, teach them to dial other numbers on your emergency phone list if the first line they call is busy.

■ Make mutual arrangements with other parents in your area that you'll aid each other's kids. Tell the children about such arrangements and introduce them to the designated adults.

■ When out with your youngsters, point out specific safe havens and safe people they could approach. Do some actual practice runs.

■ As further practice, play the "What if . . . ?" game. For instance. "What would you do if you got lost?" "What if you think you're being followed?" "What if a bigger kid threatens you?" "Then what would you do if that doesn't work?" "How about . . . [you supply an alternative]?" Emphasize what the children can *do*. Both you and your children will feel safer, and your children will feel more self-confident when they know what to do.

#43

Dealing with Strangers

In the field of protecting children from crime, no subject has received more attention than strangers. "Don't Talk to Strangers!" is the most widely promoted one-liner. Yet it isn't that simple. Recently we were at a restaurant where a wild-eyed little girl at the table next to us refused to give the waiter her order because he was a stranger.

If you and your kids are overwhelmingly concerned about *all* strangers, the youngsters will live an impoverished life and be chronic victims of their fears, whether they are ever assaulted or not.

You don't want your children to be fearful of all human beings except for the few they already know well. All the friends, coworkers, patrons, dates, lovers, and spouses youngsters ever will have during their lives will start out being strangers. Also, some types of strangers, such as police officers, store clerks, and bus drivers, are the very people to turn to for help if there is trouble.

There is another important reason your kids can't focus only on possible threats from strangers. *In most cases of mugging, harassment, assault, rape, abuse, and even murder of children, not strangers but kids and adults the victims already knew are responsible.*

A parent therefore has to strike a balance in training youngsters about strangers. Most strangers are either safe and potentially helpful or indifferent; only a small minority pose a real threat. So children have to learn to screen them and learn to stay protected while doing so.

Children need to be wary of strangers who do not clearly belong to the "helpful" groups, or those whom they encounter in isolated, unsupervised situations where no other grown-ups are around. And even when the strangers seem okay—a solicitous store clerk or the other kids in a scout group they just joined—youngsters should be alert until these unknown persons have proven themselves trustworthy. Your kids will be in the business of assessing strangers all of their lives (as you and we still are). In a sense, because of the world in which we all live, every new person must be regarded as "guilty until proven innocent." The sections that follow give many specific pointers for protecting kids from dangerous strangers, but here are some first steps.

■ Through your own example and supervision, train your children to meet new people only in public situations, preferably in a setting where there is guardianship—for instance, at a scout troop meeting, in a classroom, or through an introduction by a trusted neighbor.

■ Train your children to recognize helpful types of strangers, such as police officers, teachers, dental hygienists, waitresses, clerks—people on the job. But they should stay alert, follow their gut feelings, and talk to you about it if anything "weird" happens. One good rule of thumb is that strangers they approach for help are safer than strangers who approach them.

■ Teach them to avoid situations where they would be alone with strangers under unsupervised conditions, such as on a deserted playground or walking home alone.

■ Remember to downplay the risks. Making children chronically fearful of strangers often can do as much long-term damage to their lives as an actual assault.

#44

Out to Play

The first thing most children do "on their own" is to go out to play. This point marks the beginning of something that should continue for as long as they are living under your roof. You always need to know where your kids are (*Mega-Strategy One, "Keep in Touch"*). Having them accountable to you for their whereabouts has both a disciplinary and a security aspect. You'll need some of the discipline to help maintain their security.

How much freedom you give your children and when depends on your neighborhood and on the children's maturity and responsibility levels. Child development studies show that, over time, children's boundaries gradually widen, based on a complex give-and-take with parents, and much trial and error. Don't be too hasty in turning your children loose without checking on how they're doing. At the same time, you don't want to be a jailer.

Toddlers should always be accompanied. Slightly older children might play in your secured outside area, such as a fenced-in backyard. School-age children should be accompanied when going beyond your yard, at least by another youngster if there is any significant level of crime in your area. They should be taught early to remain in public view and to avoid isolated locations, such as abandoned buildings, overgrown gullies, or secluded woods. And they should be taught to screen and handle strangers, including other kids they don't know.

As children grow older they will range farther and farther

from home. As they do so, the two main potential situations to contend with are theft of their toys and other belongings, and harassment or assault of some kind upon them personally.

For their possessions, your best tactic is to supervise children's securing of them from an early age, and check that they have done so. Losing a favorite tricycle or stuffed animal may be what's necessary to bring the lesson home; it happened to most of us. Your aim is for children to learn to safeguard their belongings habitually, like second nature. As in the development of any skill, repetition is the key.

Carelessness is children's chief mistake with their possessions. They forget to grab their raincoat when they dash to change buses; they leave their bike parked unattended out on the walk when they run in to the bathroom; they leave their books on the bench when they go meet someone at the playground. This carelessness just has to be trained out of them, by your own example and supervision, and perhaps by hard direct experience. Angry verbal admonitions or heaping blame on children seems to be the least effective tactic.

Even when children take the utmost care, belongings still can be stolen, but with training in vigilance the odds are drastically reduced.

Most of the tactics outlined in the last chapter and the remaining pages bear on your children's personal security. Of them all, *Mega-Strategy Four, "Go Public,"* is the most crucial.

You should personally check out any play areas, such as nearby playgrounds and parks, before allowing young children to go there. Keep an alert eye even on your immediate neighborhood, and be sure children know well what to do in case of trouble. Know who they are playing with, and if you have any doubts about a child's influence, refuse to allow your children to play with him or her.

Your children probably will be invited to play with other kids, go on little trips, and go to birthday parties. Be sure they know your name, phone number, and address. (You can sew it inside their clothing.) Check to be sure there is adequate supervision for any such outings or parties. Don't hesitate to phone the other youngsters' parents and ask. These little extra steps on your part significantly increase your child's protection.

#45

Going to and from . . .

As your children venture out on their own, they do a lot of going *to* and *from*—a playmate's house, the park, school, the store, and so on. During these to-and-from transits, they are potentially more vulnerable.

One thing parents sometimes don't realize is how easily children can lose their way. It is important to walk with them along the route several times, showing them how to go and where *not* to go. After a couple of times you can have the children be the "guide" and lead the way, so you can see how they do and make any corrections. (Don't forget to praise them for doing well.)

Whenever possible, have the children go in the company of other children or adults. This is especially true if it is night or even getting near dusk.

Whether they are with someone or alone, children should be taught to stay on populated routes and refrain from any shortcuts through isolated locations. Overgrown foliage and landscaping along the way should be given a wide berth. It is also good to explain to them *why* they should avoid isolated spots, without scaring them unduly.

Teach your youngsters to recognize the "safe havens" along their routes. These are far more numerous than you might at first think. Fire stations, the post office, the homes of family friends, a neighborhood store, a fast food place you go to, a well-populated bus stop can all be safe shelters. Many neighborhood crime-prevention groups establish "safe houses" where kids (or grown-ups) can go in an emergency. The National

Crime Prevention Council has established tens of thousands of "McGruff Houses" across the country, identified by the McGruff symbol, where any child in trouble can go. Any trusted person they know, even an older kid, also can be a source of aid. Show them where public telephones are along their routes and teach them how to use one.

If children are approached by unidentified strangers, they should ignore them and keep walking. In most cases this will handle the situation. Any heckling or obscenities also should be ignored. If there are several kids or suspicious-looking characters loitering up ahead, children should cross the street or duck into a safe haven. If such a loitering situation persists, you should tell neighbors and the police so that the potential troublemakers can be checked out. If children are harassed persistently, a parent or older sibling can accompany them for a while, find out what's going on, and take remedial action.

Children should be taught to stand well away from any car that stops to ask questions or engage in conversation. It is especially important to stay well back from unidentified vans. Don't display kids' names on clothing, such as T-shirts, because a would-be assailant can pretend to know them by calling out their name.

If children feel that they are being followed, train them to duck into a safe haven, if one is close, or head immediately for a busy, populated area. If nothing else, they should yell and run. If the person bothering them is in a motor vehicle, they can turn and run in the direction *opposite* the traffic flow, which makes it almost impossible for the vehicle to stay alongside them.

If children run into "petty" mugging, the advice of all crime experts is the same as that given previously in Strategy 37, "On the Spot." Give the muggers what they want with no fuss or argument and get away as quickly as possible. And tell them to always report the incident.

Use the "What if?" game once again. Ask your kids: "What if somebody stopped a car and said, 'Come here, kid.' " "What if two older boys seemed to be following you?" "What if a guy blocked your path and said, 'Gimme that watch and your money or I'll break your arm?' " You will probably get some fanciful answers, such as "I'd give him a karate chop to the nose," but that's okay. Just keep it a game. Let children keep coming up with alternatives, while you gently steer them to more effective ones.

#46

Choosing Day Care and Preschool

If you are a working single parent or if both parents work, you will probably rely on day care and preschool. This isn't a disaster because the research shows that day-care kids are no worse off than kids raised solely by a loving mother at home—as long as the day-care kids were given parental supervision. Yet centers vary tremendously in the quality of service they render. You need to first check possible centers out thoroughly, and second, listen closely to what your youngsters say about their experiences there once they start.

No doubt you will have questions about a center's programs, lunches, snacks, and so on. Here the focus is on security.

■ Check to see that a prospective center is legally certified. Certification does not guarantee a child's safety, because states vary widely in their standards and in whether they enforce the regulations. But certification will help protect you from the most flagrant substandard situations.

■ Ask other parents about the centers in your area. *Also* ask the attending kids. But don't *rely* only on their responses.

■ Check the centers out personally. Interview the caregivers and ask questions. Are references and previous employment of the staff checked? Are they willing to have you drop by any time, unannounced? What are the security precautions against petty thefts and assaults by other children? How are the premises secured from outside interlopers? When kids go outside, how is good security maintained?

■ Visit the center during regular working hours. Compare

the interview answers you got with what you see. Chat with some of the staff and kids to get a sense of their moods and the center's emotional atmosphere. Are the attending children cheerful, or do they seem sullen and secretive? Consult your gut feelings—would *you* want to be there several hours a day? If in doubt, don't enroll your children, whatever the center's reputation.

■ Whatever center your children attend, establish the firm, inflexible rule with both center personnel and the children that no one can take them from the premises without your express permission. (Some parents establish a secret code word that any adult must know in order to pick them up.)

■ Once you are *tentatively* satisfied with a center and your children start attending, don't just leave it at that. Ask regularly how it's going and listen to what your youngsters say. There will probably be spats with other kids and ill humor toward some staff member who won't indulge them—these "go with the territory." Don't be overprotective; your children do have to learn to handle the outside world. But if in doubt, dig in and find out.

Mega-Strategy One, "Keep in Touch," will help you decide when complaints are merely squabbles, when they should be looked into further, and when they should be acted on immediately. What you are checking for is gross negligence, any abuse, or criminality.

Use these same tips in evaluating summer camps. Check with other parents and *especially* with kids who've been there. The American Camping Association has set up stringent standards for accrediting camps. You can call them and inquire toll free: 1 800 428–CAMP.

#47

School Security Tips

Kindergarten sometimes has been whimsically called "academic bootcamp," where youngsters are indoctrinated with the rules and realities of the academic game. Your children's school experiences probably will be quite a bit different from what yours were. Schools have not all turned into blackboard jungles. But school crime has risen, so kids need to be more alert and parents more vigilant than in bygone days.

We know the circumstances in which most school crime occurs, and, no surprise, our seven mega-strategies go a long way in thwarting them. Because you can't be there directly, you'll need to depend on your training and your youngsters' own developing savvy. Here are pointers to stress to your kids:

- Stay with the crowd physically. Stay around other students and staff and avoid isolated sections of the buildings and grounds. The presence of other students and staff deters troublemakers.
- Report anything worse than incidental trouble to a teacher, the principal, school nurse, or other staff member, and you.
- Steer clear of kids who bring any weapons to school or who are involved with drugs in any way. It is also best to not take sides in any fights that break out.
- Don't linger alone in the building or playground after school. A child who is staying late for any reason should be picked up or otherwise brought home safely. Teach your children what you want them to do if they miss the bus or their ride.

■ Walk to and from school with others or at least in full public view.

■ Never accept rides from unidentified persons. Never accept a ride from anyone who says a parent sent them, unless the parent specifically said so beforehand. Child Find, Inc., recommends using a secret family code word.

■ Tell parents about clearly criminal activities such as drug dealing or persistent violence. (Together with other parents, you can then decide what to do—perhaps reporting it anonymously to school authorities and the police.)

■ Try to use restrooms only when there are others around, for instance, during class breaks.

■ Keep close track of belongings. Lock lockers, don't give out the combination, and don't leave possessions unattended "for just a minute." Petty thievery is one of the most common crimes, from elementary on up through graduate school.

■ Strive to get along (*Mega-Strategy Seven*). This doesn't in any way mean being a doormat. It does mean not needlessly aggravating other children and grown-ups or creating ill-will through gossip and backbiting. A friendly network of chums and acquaintances can be a portective umbrella.

■ Get to know as many schoolmates as possible. Studies show that kids are less likely to pick on those they know even slightly.

There probably have never been children who didn't get into some trouble at school—sometimes as victims, sometimes as co-conspirators or even instigators—and your temptation may be to jump in and handle everything when your kids do. Yet children *have* to learn to cope with their surroundings; there is no way you can always run interference for them. Besides, if you solve all their problems for them, they won't be learning their own problem-solving skills.

So you don't want to overprotect them when they run into

"minor" taunting and bullying, for instance. Yet you need to be their guardian if things get out of hand. They will be teased (weren't you?) and maybe exploited a bit by older kids, and they'll run into some situations they feel timid and fearful about. In this imperfect world, these things are virtually inevitable.

Whether to intervene or not? Ask your children; listen to what they say, and if possible, let them decide if they want help. Often they don't; they just want to talk it out. Keep in mind that what might seem like petty incidents, no big deal to you, might loom as a very big deal for your kids.

Get to know your children's teachers and keep in touch with them. Ask the teachers how your youngsters are doing, but don't automatically take either side if there's a squabble. Talking openly with both teachers and your kids can be an effective check and balance on both of them.

If you need to put pressure on the school, it is much more effective for two or more parents to confront school authorities together. Giving yourselves a name, such as "The ——— Street Parents Group," will give your concerns a lot more weight. If your children encounter a persistent problem in school, raise hell about it and keep on it. Concerned parents have discovered that perseverance is the most important and effective single tactic in correcting problem situations.

#48

School Buses and Mass Transportation

A few precautions make riding school buses or mass transit systems relatively secure for kids. Probably the best, easiest way to teach your youngsters is to ride with them a few times.

Sit near the driver or conductor if at all possible. The back of the bus or empty subway cars are where the most mischief occurs.

If children ride regularly, getting to know the driver is an excellent idea. For instance, you can walk your youngsters to the school bus the first few times and introduce them to the driver. It might sound corny, but it doesn't hurt at all to give the driver small treats or gratuities when holidays come around.

Teach your children not to exchange sarcasms with rowdy youths or adults. If the rowdiness persists, teach them to tell the driver or at least sit up close to him or her.

Your children should avoid deserted bus and subway stops. They should use busy ones, even when it means walking a little farther. Especially if the route involves high-crime areas, they should try not to use public transport at all after dark.

Complacency plays into a thief's hand. Sometimes children can doze off or wander mentally while riding trains and buses. If they miss their stop and end up in unknown territory, be sure they know how to spot and use safe havens and public telephones to call for help.

Everyone needs to keep a close hold on his or her possessions while riding school or public transit. A purse or book bag should be held close to the body, zipped or buttoned, and packages should be held on the lap. Transit thieves most commonly grab a purse or package and dash out the rear exit.

Crime experts recommend that you do not attach names or addresses to children's keys. That way, if they are stolen along with a purse or backpack, or if they are found by unsavory characters, a home burglary won't follow.

#49

Bicycle Security

For most youngsters, bicycles are marvelous possessions that give them a lot of pleasure and also greatly increase their mobility. Their reach becomes miles instead of just blocks. Yet theft is a constant threat. Not everyone has had a bike stolen, but everyone probably knows somebody who has.

The good news is that a few habits, consistently followed, can virtually eliminate this risk.

According to the Redondo Beach police department in California, there are two main types of bicycle thieves. The first is made up of youngsters who want a bike of their own, at least for a few minutes. In many cases they will just joy ride for a bit, then dump the bike somewhere. The second type of thief is a member of an organized bicycle theft ring.

Thwarting both types of perpetrators is simple. A locked and chained bike is very likely to remain in the hands of its owner; an unsecured bike can be gone in a few seconds. Especially in public places, bike thieves rely on speed, so any simple bike lock almost ensures security when youngsters are out riding in public. Very few thieves carry the tools necessary to pick a lock or cut through even a modest chain. Almost all bicycle stores and hardware stores carry such chains and locks, and they cost only a few dollars.

A theft can happen in a couple of seconds, which is something every bike-owning child should know. One ten-year-old whose bike was stolen said, "I just ran in to get a candy bar." He was less than ten feet away, in an open newsstand doorway, when the thief jumped on his unlocked bike and raced away.

A stolen bicycle can be a heart-wrenching experience for a child, even when the dollar value isn't high. If your child's bike is stolen, don't berate the child about what was done wrong—he or she is probably already deeply upset. Let the child express the grief, and support him or her with understanding and a hug or two. Later on, when the child has settled down, you can get together as partners and work out avoiding a recurrence in the future.

With a bicycle, youngsters can reach areas much farther from home. Some of these areas will be safe and some not so safe, so it is important to check the areas out and steer children away from the riskier ones. One excellent idea is to ride along with children at least a few times so they will learn good bike security habits directly from your own actions. If you can't ride along, strongly encourage your children always to ride with other youngsters.

■ Always clearly mark your child's bike with an I.D. number and check with the local police if it is stolen. There's a fair chance you'll get it back.

■ Train your children always to lock up a bike when not actually riding it.

■ A bike will be even more secure if it is chained to a bike rack, pole, or other immovable object.

■ A bike should be both locked and put in the garage or back porch when not in use.

■ If a child has a bike stolen, support him or her with compassion, and work out a game plan for getting it replaced.

■ If possible, bike ride with your children or have them ride with another person. Two people are always much safer than one.

- Teach your children not to ride in high-crime or isolated areas.
- For both accident safety and crime-security reasons, it is strongly recommended that you don't let children go riding after dark.

#50

Malls, Movies, and Munchies

Youngsters going off on their own to a shopping center, a movie, or even a nearby fast food outlet can run into a whole different set of problems than when they go with you. Their chances of getting into trouble are magnified, unless they follow security guidelines faithfully.

If it is at all possible, it is always best for a child to go with someone else, at least an older sibling or another child. But the companion also has to show a level of responsibility. You need to curb any tendencies for the two children to egg each other on, which could lead to their getting into mischief. Some parents have come up with the tactic of having a baby-sitter take a youngster on such outings, or they pay another child's expenses so their child won't be alone.

Before kids are allowed to go alone, they must demonstrate enough self-care responsibility that you can *count on* them following your rules. You need to be sure they will adhere strictly to the "Going to and from . . ." (Strategy 45) guidelines and that they always stay in public view. Children won't always mind a parent. (Did you?) But even when they act up or loiter, they need to know enough not to drop all their security habits.

When they go is almost as important as *if* they go. Nighttime, especially on weekends, should be nixed if they'll be alone, until they reach their teens.

It is advisable not to let your kids go somewhere they haven't been before, unless they are with a trusted adult. They won't know the lay of the land, which makes them more vulnerable.

Youngsters usually push to have more freedom, yet parents

need to be cautious about extending such freedom. And there's no reason to be stampeded just because "other kids" get to do something. Other kids, at least some of them, may be running wild from neglect. Follow your own counsel.

When they are without adult supervision in public places, your children need to:

- Stay where other people are around and avoid secluded back areas.
- Move away from any rowdy groups and any disputes that break out among patrons.
- If approached sexually, move away and immediately tell a manager, usher, clerk, or security officer.
- Adhere strictly with no deviation from the agreed-upon arrangements for getting back home. And adhere strictly to the prearranged backup plan if stranded.
- Scream and yell, "This is not my parent!" if they are grabbed by anyone.

Millions of kids safely go to malls, stores, and fast food outlets every day, so don't be overanxious—just be prudent.

#51

Halloween

Recently one of our children, now in his twenties, sighed and said, "Halloween just isn't what it used to be." For one thing, there have been several highly publicized horror stories about poison and razor blades being put in the children's treats. Although these incidents are actually *very rare*, they have happened. Children also have been robbed of their sacks of goodies by older youths. And the streets after dark now demand more caution.

Parents across the nation have responded by taking some prudent measures that are good advice.

Trick-or-treating kids should be accompanied at all times by an adult who stays with them and stands nearby when they knock on doors. The adult should stand at the bottom of the steps or the head of the walk, visible to the person who opens the door. It's also important to have a reliable flashlight along, so no one is stumbling in the dark.

All treats should be inspected before being consumed; risks are very slight, but it's still worth doing.

Many parents now take their children only to homes in their neighborhood network. The children still get enough treats for a self-indulgent feast, without foraying into unknown neighborhoods. Other parents have a party at their or a neighbor's house for the local children. That way the kids still can wear costumes and gorge themselves, but under supervised, secure conditions.

At a minimum, have your youngsters go with other children, have a responsible "designated leader," set time limits, and set geographical limits on where they can go.

During the Halloween season it is also prudent to take a few steps to thwart mischievous pranksters and vandalism. Thoroughly inspect your exterior grounds with an eye toward minimizing temptations. (Youngsters can get good hands-on experience by helping you with this.) Store all lawn furniture, garden tools, toys, barbecue grills, and other items safely under lock and key. Also, don't leave garbage cans out. Park your car inside a secured garage, if possible; if not, see that it is locked and parked in a well-lighted spot. Illuminate your property well, especially back and side lights, and suggest your neighborhood network do the same; a well-lighted neighborhood discourages vandals and thieves. These measures also make it safer for the trick-or-treaters themselves.

#52

"Latchkey Kid" Security

If you had your way you might never, regularly, leave your kids home on their own. But career or economic necessities might force you to do so. If you are in this situation, feeling guilty about it won't help anyone. And there's no reason it has to be a disaster. Studies show that the latchkey experience can be a positive one and that a parent's working is harmful only if there is a drastic reduction in supervision and communication—only if kids are not given adequate supervision and emotional support. Overall, latchkey kids are as well adjusted as those going home to a parent or baby-sitter. You can take effective steps to help ensure that your latchkey child remains crime free.

■ Experts strongly recommend that you learn about the latchkey arrangement, its positive sides and pitfalls. Talk with parents from your network who are doing it. Read up on it, but steer clear of sensationalist articles. An excellent, balanced reference is Lynette and Thomas Long's *The Handbook for Latchkey Children and Their Parents.*

■ Thoroughly check out possible alternatives in your local area to having your children come home to an empty house. A rapidly growing number of schools, YMCAs, Boys and Girls Clubs of America, libraries, and so on are now offering supervised, constructive activities to fill after-school time. Ask your network, local school personnel, and local youth groups for leads.

■ Evaluate honesty whether your children are mature enough yet to handle the latchkey experience. Do they habitually follow security tactics? Do they mind you pretty well or habitually disobey and get into scrapes? Can they easily use your locks and any alarm system? Is your parent-child interpersonal bridge in good shape? In making your decision, talk it over with your youngsters, explain why you are considering it, and listen to their feedback. Several such talks may be advisable. If you have real doubts, however, try to make other arrangements until your children mature a bit.

■ If you decide on the latchkey option, you need to establish clear rules. Yet your rules need to be explained and discussed, not just laid down, if you want them followed. These rules should include the pointers from earlier sections, such as not letting any strangers in. It's best to write out the rules clearly and display them along with the emergency phone numbers. *Include addresses and numbers where you can be reached at all times*. Be positive by showing and saying that you think they can handle the responsibility.

■ Continue to "*Keep in Touch*" (*Mega-Strategy One*). Surveys show that the most common complaint among latchkey kids is that parents become "too busy and too tired" to share communication. When former latchkey youngsters were asked what would have made the experience better, "more communication" was by far the most frequent response.

Keeping in touch can be done in many different ways. Some parents leave a "Welcome Home" note or snack for the children arriving back from school. Others arrange for an automatic check-in call to make sure all is okay and chat for a minute or two. Child experts also strongly recommend quality time in the evening and on weekends, when you can share the adventures and hassles each of you had while you were apart.

■ Make sure you "childproof" dangerous items as well as your own private things. There's a very good chance that youngsters will snoop, so you'll need to secure medicines, any guns or Mace, and your private papers, diary, and the like.

Look around; are there things such as condoms, a vibrator, or contraceptive pills that you don't want to talk with your kids about right now?

■ You'll have to contend with the "cat's away, mice will play" possibilities. Children may bring their friends into the home, horse around, or experiment sexually while home without adult supervision. (The majority of young girls who lose their virginity do so after school at someone's house.) Confessions about such things turn up frequently in counseling sessions. So don't be totally dismayed if some mischief comes to light. One excellent suggestion is occasionally to go home early and unannounced. Praise or retrain the children, depending on what you find. Remember that they *are* kids; don't hold them to impossible standards.

■ Youngsters should be given a plan for handling any threats or fears, real or imagined, while taking care of themselves. Try to arrange places close by where they can go and people they can phone. Write the numbers on the emergency phone list—and be sure to include people who ordinarily are home. If there's no immediate threat, but children feel anxious, more and more communities are instituting "warm lines" where kids can phone and talk problems over with a trained volunteer. Check to see if your area has one.

■ If you have several children and the older one is responsible for the others, the older one has double responsibility. In effect, he or she is baby-sitting, with all that this involves. So talk it out with the older child before you impose such an arrangement. As he or she has what amounts to a part-time job, reward the child for it too.

■ The child's housekey should not be worn on a visible chain. This advertises that the kid will be home alone. A concealed chain or inside pocket is best. A spare key can be left, with prior arrangement, with a neighbor.

■ If children even suspect they are being followed, and no

one else is home, they should not go to their home. They should go immediately to any safe haven instead and contact the police or adults on their emergency list. Also, as noted earlier, if it looks as if there's been a break-in, youngsters should never go inside your dwelling. They should go to a safe haven to call you and the police instead.

■ All the tips from the Strategy 28, "Safely Home Alone," and Strategy 45, "Going to and from . . . ," should be reviewed and followed.

#53

Missing Child

The fear of having a kidnapped or missing child haunts the minds of many parents, fueled in part by graphic media stories. But, believe it or not, we have quite a bit of good news on the subject.

First of all, the earlier estimates about kidnapping rates have proven to be wildly exaggerated. The cases that do occur are often heartrending, but there may be no more than perhaps a few hundred violent kidnappings by strangers each year, which makes child abduction one of the least likely crime hazards. Whatever the precise figure is, it is one of the rarest crimes against children.

By far the largest percentage of "kidnappings" are actually "child-snatchings" by one or another ex-spouse, often in the midst of custodial squabbles. Although such incidents can be upsetting emotionally to all involved, virtually never is the child physically harmed. SEARCH, the missing child organization, roughly estimates that there may be 25,000 to 50,000 such cases annually, although it is often difficult to tell if any illegalities have been involved.

Over 98 percent of all children reported as missing are found within a few hours by the police or they turn up on their own. Usually they have gone to a friend's house or stayed at school or missed their bus stop, or stayed to play longer than they were supposed to. Virtually every parent has gone through the experience of his or her children turning up late. Law enforcement officers and crime experts emphasize, however, that parents should call the police *immediately* if a child is missing. The police have an outstanding record for finding kids who have strayed. Don't wait another half hour or so to see if kids show up. Give as accurate a description of the children as you can and include any helpful details, such as where they might be, what they were wearing, what they had been doing, and any upsets you know of. Then try to be calm; the odds are better than fifty to one you'll have the children back in no time.

It's a good idea to photograph your children every six months—clear snapshots will do—so you can provide an identifying picture if necessary.

If your children are trained in the measures for avoiding unidentified strangers, such as staying public, not standing close to a stranger's car, not hitchhiking, and not opening the door to unknown callers, their chance of being kidnapped forcibly will be reduced almost to the vanishing point.

Kids should always have emergency money for a phone call—two quarters at a minimum. Also, teach them the number for the national missing child hotline, 1 800 I AM LOST. In the unlikely event that they are abducted, they should make every effort to attract attention, get away, and contact any grown-up they can, according to kidnap experts. If any opportunity arises they should scream and yell, "This is not my parent." Many children do succeed in escaping their captors.

If you believe that your child really has been kidnapped, contact your local police and follow their instructions. If you're not listened to, speak with a higher-level officer. Also contact the national Missing Children Network at 1 800 235–3535. It is imperative that you talk with and follow the instructions of experts in this situation.

Far more children run away than are kidnapped. Strategy 75, "Preventing Runaways," explains how to handle this situation.

#54

Preventing Child Molestation and Abuse

Outside the home, there are three basic sources for sexual molestation or abuse of children: (1) other children, especially older ones; (2) adults the child is acquainted with, such as professionals treating the child, school personnel, relatives, and friends of the family; and (3) strangers who succeed in enticing the child. *Why* people molest or abuse children is a hotly debated issue with no clear answers. Sometimes molesters were themselves abused as children, but this is far from always the case.

People who are not attracted to the idea of molesting or abusing kids cannot understand why others are. So they often let their guard down with a child's teacher, dentist, or Uncle Henry. Because most offenders are people the children know, letting down your guard is dangerous—the Planned Parenthood League has found that at least three-fourths of offenders were known by the children.

In the overwhelming majority of cases, offenders use enticements, such as offers of treats, gifts, or friendship, not brute force, in violating a child. Often the touching proceeds gradually from nonsexual to sexual and more intimate, and the offenses tend to become habitual, not a one-time thing, unless stopped. Also, researcher Gene Abel and others have found that boys are almost as likely to be sexually molested as girls, although such incidents are reported even less often because of humiliation and the homosexual stigma. If a child tells you about a molestation, believe him or her; researchers have found that kids very rarely lie about this.

Molestation by strangers is the easiest to thwart. Most of the tactics outlined previously operate to make kids less available and less vulnerable. Children should also be taught to ignore and walk away from or loudly say "No!" to any sort of enticements from unidentified strangers who engage them in conversation. They should also tell a working adult, such as a teacher, security officer, or even store clerk, that a person is bothering them. These offenders are especially wary of any public attention. More times than not, child molesters already have a police record, so *they* are vulnerable.

Intimacies with other kids are more of a problem, because most children indulge in a bit of naive sexual play, such as "Doctor" or "You show yours; I'll show mine." The line between such play and exploitation is sometimes hard to draw because kids are naturally curious and often actively engage in their own exploring. Short of enrolling the kids in a monastery, you really can't stop such explorations. What you *do* want to stop is any exploitation or abuse from other kids.

Know whom your children are playing with and running around with. Ask about their friends, what they did, and so on. Try to get acquainted with all their companions—the fact that you know them, where they live, and their parents has a curbing disciplinary influence. Also, know where your young children are, whom they are with, and what they are doing. Spending time with older kids may be utterly harmless, even beneficial in a big-brother or big-sister way. But be alert for any sudden secretiveness, withdrawal from usual activities, refusal to talk, altered body language, or other changed behavior.

If an incident involving other children does occur, you can choose what to do from a range of responses, on the basis of how serious you feel the situation is. You can inform the police and make a formal complaint. You can talk it over with the other parents. You can caution your child. Or you can let it slide. If an older child is involved, we suggest as a minimum not letting your youngster see that person anymore. The possibilities of your child being taken advantage of are just too great. See Strategy 57, "Older Companions" for more on this.

Molestation by a known adult can be the most difficult situation for both children and parents. Sometimes children really like and admire the offending grown-up. Or at least the children might feel obligated to submit to hugs, tickling, and sitting on a lap because it is a relative. They may also feel they're supposed to obey their elders, professionals, and school personnel.

One excellent tactic is never to force your kids to kiss or hug or sit on the lap of grown-ups if they don't want to. This puts such behavior under their own direct control and teaches them by example that they have the right to refuse. Let them know that it is okay for them to say "Don't do that" or "I don't like that—stop it!" *to anyone.* This measure alone is half the battle in thwarting molestation from acquaintances; potential offenders almost always are very leery of public disclosure.

Often acquaintance offenders use some ploy to get children to remain silent, such as stories about terrible things that will happen if word gets out. So it is important to let youngsters know that they can tell you anything, that you'll stand by them, and that you can handle it, whatever it is. This reassurance goes far to counteract any silencing ploys a potential offender might use.

If you are a single parent who is dating, know your partners well before giving them free rein with your kids and house. Sometimes people you don't know well may have hidden pasts, or could be con artists and thieves.

Molestation often comes from members of stepfamilies and "blended families" so be alert in these situations until you're sure who's okay.

From their own accounts, convicted habitual child molesters

say they cruised to spot children who "drooped"—who showed signs of being neglected and emotionally hungry—because these kids were vulnerable to their come-ons of friendliness and gifts. Keeping in touch (*Mega-Strategy One*) and a stable home life can provide a strong bulwark against victimization.

6

Teenage Tremors

The teenage years are usually tumultuous for both parents and teenagers. Your youngsters will be going through tremendous physiological changes. They will stray farther afield as they continue to grow and explore the world. But they also can get into more trouble. This chapter helps you help your children safely navigate the adolescent period.

This chapter does not cover all the ins and outs of raising teenagers. Having raised several of them, we concur with the English essayist John Wilmot: "Before I got married I had six theories about bringing up children; now I have six children and no theories." Former president Harry S Truman put it more whimsically: "I have found the best way to give advice to your children is to find out what they want and then advise them to do it." We can't tell you all about raising teens, but we can tell you a lot about protecting them from crime.

Don't be fooled by your youngsters' angry disagreements, sullen looks, and defiant statements. You are still the major continuing influence in the adolescents' life, and you can use this influence to help keep your children crime free. Situations will arise when your kids will have to make decisions, often on-the-spot ones, about drugs, alcohol, shoplifting, aggression, and sex. While you almost certainly won't be there when those times of decision occur, your influence will.

#55

Keeping the Line Open

Maintaining fairly open communication with your growing teenagers is the only effective way to know what is happening with them. It is also the most reliable way to have some *influence* over what they do. It will probably take some extra effort on your part, yet most experts agree that open parent-child communication is the single most important factor in keeping adolescents out of crime's way.

Even before the onset of puberty, your kids will have formed some strong opinions of their own that are likely to differ quite a bit from yours. They are growing up in a world different from the one you did, and, after all, they are also different people. So your communications skills are likely to be put to the test, and you won't always be successful. Some of your cherished beliefs and values may be open questions for them, while some of their notions may be shocking to you.

Hang in there. On many things you also can agree to disagree with them, without damaging your precious interpersonal bridge.

It's fine to disagree about some rock star or a hairstyle, but keep in mind that *you are still in charge and there have to be rules*. The rules can do much to help protect your child. Rules, such as a curfew, should be clear, understood, and used. Kids *need* to be somewhat accountable for what they do.

You can't raise children without discipline, just as you can't drive a car unless you steer it. If the rules are not enforced at all, they aren't rules. The rules should have a bit of flexibility in them, for instance, staying out later on special occasions. And when they are broken (which they will be), children should be able to get off the hook without too much trauma. Also, the rules should be open to some negotiation and modification as time goes on. Give-and-take discussions can be very helpful.

In these negotiations, however, remember that as Phyllis York, David York, and Ted Wachtel point out in their excellent book, *ToughLove*, you and your kids are *not* equal. Nor—despite the parade of pop psychology theories—are you to blame every time your child is a brat or gets in trouble. Don't let your kids or the latest celebrity family therapist bully you about not being a perfect parent. No parents are saints, and almost all the saints never had kids.

Besides, who has ever seen a perfect kid?

The rules should have rewards as well as punishments. Your own job experiences have probably shown you how important this can be. Because adolescents always want something, it isn't hard to work out rewards. An atmosphere of good fellowship can be one of the most important assets for weathering these years.

An open communication line will give you the channel for letting your growing youngsters know how you feel about drugs, sex, underage drinking, hitchhiking, new companions, and so on. And their feedback on these issues can help to keep you abreast of what's going on in their heads and their lives.

Teens are almost bound to become moody and go silent now and then, and it may be hard to open them up. Try to get them talking about innocuous things with you; what's really bothering them will often then pop out a little later. The silences usually will pass. If silences persist, ask directly, "What's going on?" The kids may be fooling with drugs or sex, as we'll see. "*Keep in touch*" with yourself too. If you're having a rough time with your teens, talk it out with friends, confide in a personal journal, or join a parent support group.

Remember: You can never control your youngsters entirely. You can't stop them from doing illegal things or taking stupid risks if that's what they decide to do. But you can educate them, train them, support them, provide opportunities for them, and influence their decisions if the line of communication is open.

#56

Peer Pressure — The Hidden Persuaders

There is good news and bad news about peer pressure. The bad news is that most teenagers break the law in the company of other teenagers. Also, most teenagers who are victimized are done unto by their teen peers. The good news is that peer pressure can be positive, supportive, and along the lines you approve of. *So the net effects of peer pressure on your youngsters depend on the "peers" and the "pressures."*

Whether they use the term "peer pressure" or not, the thing that worries parents most are these outside influences on what their kids think, how they feel, and what they do—and this concern is justified. Gang violence, drug damage, teen pregnancies, and sexually transmitted diseases are real facts of life. Yet, despite lurid media portrayals, not every new companion of your youngsters is likely to be a sexually promiscuous, drug-abusing cultist. Happily, only a small minority of teenagers are really unrelenting "bad influences." Most are just uncertain, suggestible, and a bit rebellious.

By the teenager years, your children will have developed something of their own personal life-style, based partly on your influences and the opportunities you have provided. This personal life-style is very important because it plays such a large part in determining whom they associate with and whom they don't. Without being moralistic, it is simply true that some life-styles are more wholesome and less crime prone than others. A science club, a music group, a church youth group, team sports, or a college-prep program certainly are going to lead your youngsters to meet different people from a street gang or cult.

The same thing applies to influences from older people; a piano teacher is a better bet than a school dropout.

Encouraging and steering your teens toward crime-free interests and activities is far more effective than elaborate sets of rules or stern lectures. Such supportive steering is the single biggest influence parents can have on what kinds of peer pressures their children will experience. A wide range of such relatively wholesome opportunities is available everywhere, although it may take a bit of work to discover them. Aside from our generic mega-strategies, noncriminal associations and activities are the best safeguard against your kids being victimized or drifting into illegalities.

Let youngsters do the final choosing—they will anyway. You can *suggest,* facilitate, negotiate, and support, but imposing isn't very effective. If adolescents want to play the guitar, giving them violin lessons probably won't work.

The fact that adolescents are fickle in their relationships and interests drives some parents half crazy. Today's bosom friend becomes tomorrow's archenemy, and the got-to-have computer game set sits in the closet gathering dust when youths switch their focus to school plays. Teens are changing rapidly and trying out new things, so this fickleness is natural. It's important to keep in touch with these changes, rather than throw up your hands, because you are more likely to catch early warning signs of careless behavior or dangerous drifts.

Continue the practice of knowing where they are, who they're with, and what they are doing—this maintains your psychological "presence" even when you're not physically there. Teenagers often get touchy about parental prying and interference, but you can point out, rightfully, that you are their guardian until they come of age and are out on their own—and you're paying the bills. If you continue to let them know where *you* are and what *you're* doing, your inquiries will be more acceptable. Also, let them know you care.

Meet their friends and dates, their teachers, aerobics instructor, and so on. This also puts your psychological "presence" on the line, which often curbs wayward behavior. And you will be in a better position to see that new friends don't breech the family security habits you've established.

Adolescent culture has something of a natural antiparent component to it, and teens sometimes will conspire together against their folks. Teens sometimes also use prevailing pop psychology theories, such as calling their family "dysfunctional," in an effort to excuse their own misbehavior. They may exaggerate or even lie about negative aspects of their home life. Unfortunately, school and youth counselors sometimes buy these false stories and side with the kids to the point that parents become guilt-ridden and intimidated. No family is perfect; most do the best they can. From what we've seen, most parents are unsung heroines and heroes. A small minority of families truly are dysfunctional, but the majority are not. And "parent abuse" can be as destructive of family stability as child abuse. An unruly brat is an unruly brat, who does not have the inalienable right to destroy a family structure.

Without being domineering or authoritarian, you may need to take firm stands with children. From the cases we've seen, truly unacceptable behavior swiftly becomes illegal and self-destructive behavior that eventually can pull an entire family down. Unless you take firm stands, back them up, and stick to them, you "subsidize" waywardness and ill-treatment of yourself.

Despite their sophisticated posing, adolescents are still quite naive and vulnerable. They are, for instance, usually very innocent about economic realities, about what's involved in maintaining a household, and about how to manage relationships. They are standing on shifting ground, with one foot in childhood and the other in adulthood, and they do need your guidance to remain crime free.

You may despair over whom your kids admire and want to be like, but if you can hold on, they probably will change their minds again, next week or next month.

#57

Older Companions

Your teens will be associating with many people who are older than they are. Two things distinguish such relationships. The older persons are more knowledgeable, and (more important) they usually have more power, prestige, and resources. Even a youngster three years older than yours might have a car, more money, and more savvy. Such older people can serve as role models, can inspire, and can provide new opportunities for your growing youngsters.

Yet counseling files reveal that there is sometimes a darker side to such influences. Older companions sometimes use their position to seduce or exploit youngsters. The seduction or exploitation can take many forms. Youths may be led, step by step, into various sexual practices. They might be introduced to drugs or alcohol. They might be exploited work-wise or financially. They might be inducted into a gang or cult. They might be converted to attitudes and life-styles that are in marked opposition to those of your family.

Most governments have enacted laws, such as those on statutory rape and contributing to the delinquency of a minor, to thwart such exploitations. Yet anyone who has been around knows that these laws and rules are enforced only in the most flagrant cases or in cases that are organizationally embarrassing, such as when a high school scandal hits the media.

So what can you do to protect your kids from these kinds of threats?

Teaching your kids early on that they have the right to say no and when to say no is your first line of defense. Train them not to be cowed or overawed by older people, although they might respect and admire them. The less emotionally vulnerable kids are, the less seducible they will be.

Once again, keeping in touch is important for two reasons. First, it gives you early warnings of any "tilt" in such relationships. And second, if your children have open access to you, they will be far less likely to go elsewhere for the communication and support they want. Then their outside relationships with older people are likely to be healthy expansions instead of unhealthy substitutes.

It is an excellent practice to meet the older people in your youngsters' life, especially the ones who become important to them. Your parental "presence" is then a real live thing, not just a vague abstraction. This is no guarantee against unwanted influences, but it will help. An older person also sometimes can become an ally in helping you straighten your kids out if they start drifting toward delinquency. As a bonus, you might get to know a worthwhile person.

Letting your daughter date an older guy is chancy. You probably wouldn't be able to stop them from seeing each other if they are determined, but if you disapprove of him you can be firmly discouraging. This might at least cut the length and intensity of the relationship. There are exceptions to this caution; many girls marry or have honorable liaisons with men who are a few years older, so you'll have to use your own judgment. But realize that if they go together, they are more likely to become sexually involved than kids the same age would. The greater the age difference, the more dependent and suggestible the younger person in a relationship tends to be.

If things look as if they are getting out of hand for any reason in your youngster's relationship with an older person, you have other options. You can forbid the teen to see the person. This might or might not work, but either way you'll probably have to do some repairing of your parent-child interpersonal bridge. You can contact the older person, asking him or her to stay away, and even threaten further action if the person does not. This too, might or might not be effective, and will probably upset your youngster. Only you can decide whether to use these stronger options. In extreme cases, you can contact the authorities directly and turn the offending person in if there have been clear illegalities.

If youngsters get into trouble or get hurt because of a relationship with someone older, be there for them. Help them weather it. Don't indulge them or cover for them, but don't rub it in either. They need a friend more than anything else, so strive to be one.

#58

Forbid Hitchhiking

One word covers what your kids need to learn about hitchhiking. *Don't!* They should never hitchhike, and when they begin driving, they should never pick up hitchhikers. Also, they should discourage any drivers they ride with from picking up hitchhikers. Hitchhiking encompasses more than bumming rides on the open roads from strangers. It is also bumming rides to and from school, a dance, a party, and so on, from people they hardly know at all.

They should not accept or give rides to anyone they wouldn't trust with their body, their belongings, or their life, because that is just what they are doing. Every police department of any size has files on people who were robbed, assaulted, raped, or even murdered by hitchhikers or by those who picked them up.

Because younger teenagers cannot drive yet, they are prone to mooching rides to and from parties, school events, rock concerts, camping trips, and movies. This is understandable, but they should learn to exercise care. They should never ride with someone they feel uneasy about, who is a reckless driver, or who has been using drugs or alcohol.

By the time your youngsters begin to drive, they should have learned well from your own example to keep all car doors and windows secured to prevent sudden unwelcome intruders and not to get out of the car if flagged down by someone claiming car trouble. Rather they should offer to make a call. And as a parent, never pick up hitchhikers yourself.

To help thwart hitchhiking or accepting questionable rides, many parents tell their kids that they will pick them up from anywhere, or pay for a cab or car service home, no questions asked. Some youths report that having such an agreement with their folks makes them feel much freer to say no and more able to resist going along with peer pressure when they really don't want to.

#59

Teen Hangout Safety

Aside from school and home, teenagers are most likely to be found in hangouts, such as shopping malls, movie complexes, and areas around fast food places. Youngsters can congregate with their own age group, "cruise," girl-watch and boy-watch, shop and window shop, chow down, and just kill time. They can also drift into trouble.

Some parents try to restrict these activities by refusing permission—with only limited success. Getting adolescents involved in alternatives, such as extracurricular school programs, church youth programs, or tutoring in some skill, is usually more effective. If kids are learning a new computer program or trying out for the swimming team, they can't be wandering the mall. There is still such a thing as homework too.

Hanging out is not inherently "bad," and all kids are going to do some of it. Some psychologists could probably give us a long list of functions it serves, such as letting off steam and practicing interpersonal skills. So how can you see to it that they hang out safely?

■ Encourage your youngsters always to hang out with a companion, preferably someone you know and have confidence in. Also, they should know by now to avoid secluded sections of these public places, such as back stairways, vacant lots by the drive-in, isolated parts of the mall.

■ Curtail excessive hanging out. If it starts to be a total way of life, find out what's going on and see if you and your children can cooperatively come up with some alternatives.

■ Go with them sometimes, not as a chaperon, but as a companion. Let them show you some of their world. This will give you more exposure to their likes, feelings, and hangups, and it will help strengthen your interpersonal bridge with your teens. There is a myth that it is gauche for a teenager to be seen with parents. The truth is that many other kids are envious, as long as it's clear you're not there to spy on them. When you're out together, you can also check to see if your earlier security training is still in place.

■ You can influence the choices in both the times and the places for hanging out. All hangouts are more dangerous late at night than during after-school daylight hours. Also, the places vary widely in their crime-proneness. Don't be misled by a highly publicized incident or two; what are the routine, day-in, day-out safety levels of different hang-out spots? You can check with your parents' network and also with experienced police officers. (We, and many others, have found that law enforcement and security personnel are amazingly helpful in these kinds of inquiries, if approached politely and with respect.)

■ Work out and rehearse a concrete plan of what you want your teens to do in case an emergency arises.

■ A firmly enforced curfew is one of the most effective ways of keeping your kids out of dangerous hangouts late at night.

#60

Getting into Mischief

Teens love adventure, so it's almost certain that your kids are going to get into some mischief while growing up. This "mischief" might include petty thievery, vandalism, shoplifting, break-ins, reckless driving, underage drinking, trying drugs, truancy, or fighting.

It might be true that, as the great English writer H. G. Wells once wrote: "The crisis of yesterday is the joke of tomorrow." But you can't afford just to smile and let such mischief slide. Youngsters need to "take the fall."

If you get a call from the school that your youngsters have been AWOL, or from a department store that they were caught shoplifting, you will probably feel a confusing swirl of emotions—guilt, disbelief, embarrassment, anger, and a sense of betrayal. Such incidents are often the theme of teen comedies and prime-time sitcoms, but they're not so funny when *you* get the call.

You have to apply some discipline for two strong reasons: First, these acts, though "minor," are criminal and criminality needs discouraging. Second, such incidents often signal links with wayward companions and the possibility of more serious trouble down the line.

Whatever other discipline you apply, clearly and unequivocally show your strong disapproval. The temporary loss of a privilege or two, or some extra chores, to bring the point home won't hurt either. Also, let kids get the stern lecture from the principal, store manager, or police officer. If there's a fine, have *them* pay it.

When the dust has settled a bit, have a game plan whereby youngsters can get back in good standing with you. Don't hold a grudge—there's too much psychological evidence now on how devastating holding grudges can be for everyone concerned. But don't be a naive patsy either. You might want to institute a "probationary period" to see that the kids are now going straight. Once this period is over, let it be over.

And take heart; the vast majority of kids go through a few of these episodes, outgrow them, and come out just fine.

#61

Sex — PG, R, and X-Rated

It's no news that our society has become far more sexually explicit in the last three decades. Mainstream magazines are filled with sexual "how to" articles, rock stars routinely appear in various stages of undress, the media mention menstruation, orgasms, oral sex, rape, and homosexuality in their news coverage, and even prime-time family shows are filled with erotic innuendos. Some hail this as liberation, others see it as moral decay. However you might feel about it, it is part of the current reality that washes over our kids.

As Joel Wells points out in *How to Survive with Your Teenager*: "Your teenager is a sexual person and will be having sexual experiences of one sort or another. Parents who believe that they can shelter their children by withholding or blurring the 'facts of life' are living in a fool's paradise." Parents tend to make two misjudgments in this area. They underestimate how "sexual" their teens are, and they don't realize how naive and careless they are.

The many physiological, psychological, and moral issues surrounding sex go far beyond the scope of this book. Here we are focusing on reducing the risks of exploitation and victimization. The bottom line is that *the more naive and ill-informed youngsters are sexually, the more vulnerable they are.*

Kids want to know. Yet the Planned Parenthood League estimates that only 10 percent of students nationwide receive comprehensive sex education in their school. And seven out of ten teens report they never discussed contraception with their parents. One boy remarked, "Fear is the most common feeling people our age have about sex."

Parents and children frequently have great difficulty discussing sex, but survey after survey shows that your kids are almost certainly going to at least mess around sexually. So some kind of factual sex education is a must. Even if you don't supply it directly, you will want to supervise the content of any guidance and education your kids get.

Some sex education courses and books are so tame and superficial that youngsters just sneer at them. Other material goes so far that it is more pornographic than educational. Many good sex education books offer a range of perspectives. Your public librarian can help steer you to them. An excellent middle-of-the-road reference is the Planned Parenthood book *How to Talk with Your Child About Sexuality*, by Faye Wattleton and Elisabeth Keifer. What you should look for most is a book that clearly presents the facts.

Your youngsters need an "owner's manual" working knowledge of biological sex and how it functions in both genders. They also need to know the facts about sexual harassment, AIDS and other sexually transmitted diseases, date rape, pregnancy and its consequences. You might add to this list, but it's not prudent to delete from it. (The seven top subjects teens ask sex educators about are menstruation, wet dreams, masturbation, intercourse and pregnancy, birth control, sexually transmitted diseases, and homosexuality.)

Studies have amply demonstrated that teens tend to be more sexually active than sexually knowledgeable, which is why parental and other guidance and education is so vital. The R-rated movies and X-rated peer conversations titillate and entice far more than they inform. Often these sources foster unrealistic and distorted viewpoints. The movies, the MTV hit songs, and the locker-room talk are mostly fiction, as anyone who has had a few relationships can attest—but the kids don't really know that yet.

You can never entirely control what your kids are going to do sexually, and their sexual habits and values might end up differing markedly from yours. But they need the facts, and, if possible, open communication with you, to help protect them from exploitation, unwanted pregnancies, and serious disease, whatever moral stands you and they take.

Parents frequently ask: "When should we start educating our kids about sex?" Most experts agree, *the sooner, the better*, at least for the rudiments. That way, you can deal with their curiosity in a supervised setting. Because sexual activity and situations of all types have been drifting down the age levels, it's a good idea to have the kids pretty fully briefed by the time they are between nine and eleven.

#62

Sexual Harassment

Organizations and legislative bodies have been struggling in recent years to frame clear definitions and set clear guidelines with regard to sexual harassment—with only limited success. Difficulties stem from the fact that the term can apply to such a wide range of actions, the subject is so emotionally charged, and entrenched miscommunication between males and females is so rampant.

Sexual harassment is more about fear and intimidation than about sex. Aside from all the controversies, one thing stands out clearly. Sexual harassment involves unwanted actions that are offensive, intimidating, and emotionally upsetting for the recipient. And teens get their share of such behavior. They may encounter harassment at a part-time job, in the school hallways, during extracurricular activities, at church, or anywhere else they go. Victims are usually, but far from always, female.

Aside from any immediate upset, harassment can be a prelude to further trouble, so it is best to curb it firmly as early as possible. Luckily, rules against harassment have been made a lot tougher, and they are getting to be enforced more stringently. In other words, it is now easier to help your kids deal with this subject.

The first line of defense is conversational. If youngsters are crowded close or touched in an unwelcome way, they should say something like "Don't do that," or "I don't like that; please stop it." This should be done politely, but *very* firmly. If the harassment is verbal, they can reply firmly with such things as "I really feel put down by how you're acting." In many cases this is a surprise (and a learning experience) for the culprits, who will often stop after a strong reprimand. Perpetrators are sometimes amazed to find that their idle banter *is* harassment. The thing youngsters should not do is get pulled into a round of hostile verbal exchanges.

If these tactics don't work, the next level of response is to threaten a formal complaint. This should be done only if the earlier responses have failed to stop the harassment. If their own efforts don't seem to be getting anywhere with the offender, teens immediately should let some responsible adult know—you, a school counselor, their supervisor at work, or a security guard in a public place such as a mall. *Mega-Strategy Four: "Go Public,"* is likely to curtail any retaliation.

The extremes of harassment, such as persistent unwelcome touching or fondling, verbal obscenities, threatening demands of "sex for favors," or continuing propositions after a firm no, all warrant full formal complaints and restraining actions if necessary. Such persistent rude and insensitive behavior can too easily turn into acquaintance rape, unfair discrimination, or some kind of criminal retribution. Don't dismiss this type of behavior as "normal" when your child is involved.

Every growing youngster has probably experienced another kind of cruel harassment: taunting attacks on the youngster's masculinity or femininity. Boys who won't fight or go out for sports or who are just different are teased about being "queers" or "pussies." Girls who don't fit the current fads in beauty standards (large breasts one decade, small ones the next) are sneered at or called "dogs" or "dykes" or "fatties." There is probably no human being who has not suffered some emotional upsets at one time or another from these kinds of cutting remarks—at least the authors have never met one. Support youngsters through these trials, hear them out if they want to talk about it, and encourage them to rise above such put-downs and be themselves.

Flirtations, banter, and innuendos are part of our modern world, and most people probably would say life would be duller without them. But when they are unwelcome and unreciprocated, or threatening, they are harassment and need to be stopped.

#63

Avoiding Date Rape

If your youngsters follow certain guidelines, the risk of date rape can be virtually eliminated. Daughters, sons, and parents all need to know about these guidelines.

A girl has the fundamental human right to say no, *whatever* the situation, and have the behavior stop. Anything less constitutes rape. We would never accept a mugger's excuse that he was tempted beyond control by a well-dressed victim, or a burglar's excuse that someone with a nice house was just "asking for it." So we shouldn't accept such excuses from rapists. Ideally, a girl should be able to stay safely overnight at an army barracks, wearing see-through clothing; but this wouldn't be prudent. Our guidelines have to do with being prudent.

Because of underreporting it is difficult to get precise figures, but *at least two-thirds of all rapes and attempted rapes are not from strangers but from dates or from known acquaintances in other social settings.* Does this mean a woman has to rely upon the good manners of all her male companions to be safe? Happily, in most cases, she can; most males will accept a firm no, however grudgingly. And just a few strategies can further turn the odds dramatically in your daughter's favor.

Virtually all date or acquaintance rapes occur when the pair are alone together in some private, isolated place. A further analysis of reported incidents shows the following things: Alcohol or drugs frequently were involved, the victim had not yet gotten to know the assailant well, and some physical contact such as kissing had usually occurred. Extensive research has also documented that boy-girl miscommunications and misread signals are rampant. For instance, researcher A. Abbey found that boys very often "see" a sexual invitation when none was intended. Males generally attribute "sexiness" to a wider range of circumstances than females do. Even holding hands and a smile can be misread, let alone going to a guy's room for petting. These findings provide clues on how to avoid date rape.

Here are the essential pointers girls and young women should know and practice:

■ Stay public in early dates and social encounters until you know the guy well enough to trust him. Most date rapes happen within the first four encounters. If you see you are getting maneuvered into being alone with him, and you don't want to, bail out—the sooner the better. Males, and even other females, sometimes conspire to manipulate a situation so the couple are left alone to "make out"—unbeknownst to the girl.

■ If you begin to feel uncomfortable during a date or social encounter, listen to your hunches. Call your family or a friend, or use some excuse to get away. If you don't feel safe, refuse to ride home or to be alone with him. Date-rape cases are full of examples where the victim had strong intuitive feelings that something wasn't right, but failed to act on the feeling.

■ Stay sober. If you insist on using alcohol or drugs, pick your companions with care and realize that some males will ply you with liquor or drugs to lower your resistance and discretion. The more drunk or stoned you get, the more difficult any effective form of self-protection becomes. This point must be emphasized. Drugs or alcohol are involved in the majority of date rapes. Also, stay away from male companions who use alcohol or drugs excessively. They are bad bets in every way.

■ Be alert to the "early warning signs" of a potential acquaintance rapist. These signs, drawn from rape counselors and victims, include a belittling manner toward you; ignoring your opinions and remarks; acting in a domineering, intimidating manner; negative or cynical attitudes toward women; not treating you as an equal; hostile, resentment-laden attitudes toward the world; and anger if you don't just go along submissively with what he says and does. Even if no date rape occurs, guys who exhibit these signs are more likely to become physically or emotionally abusive if a relationship does develop.

■ Check the guy out. Unfortunately, people are often far more careful in choosing a dentist or car mechanic than they are in choosing whom they date. Talk with other girls who know him, and ask other guys too. Ask him about himself—he'll think you're a wonderful conversationalist, and you can check for the early warning signs. Talk about sex too, to get some reading of where he's at and how well his feelings fit with yours.

■ From the outset, clearly communicate what your sexual boundaries are. Don't wait until you are already on his couch embracing. Get his acknowledgment and agreement that any sexual activity will be only by mutual decision and that you have the right to say no anywhere along the line. Most people do tend to honor their explicit, up-front agreements.

■ It is extremely unwise to go off somewhere alone with a "pickup" stranger you meet at a dance or teenage hangout; you are flirting with many kinds of possible trouble. Don't let the thrill of the moment cloud your good judgment. If you are interested in him, arrange for a safe get-acquainted situation.

■ If you find yourself in a situation where you are being forced beyond your boundaries, consider freaking out. Go very visibly hysterical. Run away if you can. If people will hear you, yell and scream. "Fire" will often bring more help than "Help." If you wet yourself, vomit, defecate, you will rudely break up his erotic fantasy script and you will become a far less attractive target, which is what you want. Such displays will frighten or turn off the majority of ardent males. With acquaintances (but not strangers), it also sometimes works if you aggressively define the situation as rape.

■ Only you, in the situation, can decide about physical resistance. If the assailant is brandishing a weapon, most experts recommend against resistance. Otherwise you, the victim, must assess the circumstances and your abilities, and then decide for yourself. However, in her excellent book *I Never Called It Rape*, Robin Warshaw emphasizes that submitting does not mean consent—it is a survival act. If you do decide to resist, fight dirty and decisively to incapacitate him long enough to get away. (Aftermaths are covered in the next section.)

■ Enroll in rape prevention courses, which your local school, YWCA, or police department probably conduct. A self-defense class is also a good self-confidence builder that "telegraphs" to would-be assailants.

■ A fairly widespread "borderline" date-rape situation occurs when young girls are pushed into having sex although they don't really want to. This happens most often if a girl is infatuated with a guy and feels that she needs to give in to keep him, if there is strong "go-ahead" peer pressure, or if the girl becomes involved with an older, more sexually experienced and skilled boy. The less knowledgeable and the more emotionally vulnerable a girl is, the more powerful such pressures will be. The preceding pointers, combined with personal self-reliance and self-esteem, will go far to prevent this kind of forced sex.

If your daughter gets involved in an abusive relationship, extricating her can be tricky. The boy will probably engage in intimidation, isolation from supports, and jealous surveillance, just as in adult spouse abuse. As a first step, talk it out with an experienced worker at your local women's center.

Your youngsters of both genders should know these pointers well—they are tried and true. Your sons also should know well by your teaching and example that sex gotten by force, whether physical or emotional, or through intoxication, is legally rape. Unfortunately, our current male subculture still contains prevailing ideas about "scoring," but rape isn't macho, it's criminal.

#64

Preventing Forcible Rape

There is nothing inevitable or "natural" about rape. In a landmark cross-cultural study, anthropologist Peggy Reeves Sanday found that there were huge differences in rape rates between different societies. American women, for instance, are *several hundred times* more likely to be raped than are women in some other cultures.

It is far from inevitable that your youngsters will become rape victims, if they stay alert and follow standard security guidelines. It's not much talked about, but teen males are subject to rape too—ask any counselor—so they need to protect themselves. While it is not nearly as frequent, it does occur. Male rape is virtually always perpetrated by other males and is most likely to happen in high-crime neighborhoods, rough schools, juvenile halls, or prison settings. Young males are even more reluctant than women to report the crime, but it is as humiliating and terrifying an experience.

Most of the tactics presented in this book reduce the risks of all types of crime, and this is true for rape as well. The points about household security, going out safely, staying public, closing and locking everything, and picking your spots all apply. Being accompanied by a companion is almost as good as being accompanied by a security guard, because it has been well established from convicted offender interviews that rapists look for easy, vulnerable lone targets and usually pass by ones that present more difficulties.

Rape is an ugly subject and most of us don't want to dwell on it. Yet adolescents are "new recruits" in the wider world, so they need training in rape avoidance. Your best first move is to enroll your youngsters in a good rape prevention course at the local school, YMCA, or women's center. As a supplement to the course, teach them the following pointers:

- Keep all the home security guidelines, especially keep entrances locked, don't let unidentified strangers in for any reason, and don't let callers know you are alone.
- Jog, shop, run errands, and go to movies and parties with at least one companion whenever possible. Two are more than twice as safe as one. This isn't always possible, so when alone, stay in well-populated areas and avoid all secluded spots. Joggers are prime rape targets, so don't jog alone in secluded park, beach, or wilderness areas.
- If you feel you are being menaced or followed, don't lead the person to your home; go to a public place and get help. At least, get someone to accompany you home. Never ignore these inner promptings.
- If you hear an intruder in another part of the house, run to a neighbor if you can. If you can't, lock yourself in the safe room, make lots of noise, set off your personal alarm, and call for help. You can also turn a stereo up to speaker-shattering volume. Never confront an intruder or block his exit.
- Special care should be taken when entering and leaving places. Try to do this in the company of, or at least in sight of, others. Stay alert, even entering and leaving your own dwelling. If you sense anything out of the ordinary, take immediate security measures.
- More and more schools, commercial buildings, malls, and clinics now have escort services. Use them, especially at night.
- Don't give strangers or vague acquaintances the benefit of the doubt if they come up to you, come on to you, or are blocking your way. Stay alert and move away to a safe place.
- Follow your intuitions. If you feel uneasy or anything

seems out of the ordinary in your surroundings, act on the inner promptings and get to a safe place.

- Get an inexpensive aerosol or battery-operated personal alarm, and keep it handy when out on your own.
- Pick your spots. Rape *can* happen anywhere, but it is far more likely to happen at certain places and times, and such higher-risk situations can be avoided. For instance, stopping by a convenience store alone late at night, waiting for someone at an isolated spot, or staying late in a deserted building is not prudent. Just stay off the "mean streets" in your area.
- If grabbed or confronted by a rapist, whether to resist and what kind of resistance to put up has to be an on-the-spot decision, based on circumstances. Certainly, you should strive to escape to safety if possible. Also, if there are people around, try to attract their attention by screaming, yelling "Fire," and so on. If the assailant is armed, however, resistance may increase the danger of further harm.

Beyond these points, there is a great deal of controversy among rape and crime experts as to the best course of action. There is even much debate over the use of such nonlethal weapons as Mace; some claim it is often effective, others claim it is most likely only to enrage the assailant. Anyone who considers using such nonlethal devices should be trained and have some practice in their use.

The best way to protect your children is to prepare them. Two good ways to do this are enrolling youngsters in the rape prevention courses mentioned earlier and playing some "What if . . .?" games with them. With increased awareness and preliminary "dry-run" practice, youngsters can perceive more options in a situation and be far less likely to "freeze up" (the most common response of unprepared victims).

#65

What to Do If Rape Occurs

If your youngster is raped, stay as calm as you possibly can and focus on helping her (or him) through the situation and its aftermath. Support her unconditionally and listen to her without heaping any blame or recrimination upon her whatsoever. The *Ms.* magazine survey and other studies have shown that teenagers often fail to even tell their families they have been raped because they fear the family will blame them, and because they may have been involved in misconduct, such as underage drinking, at the time. She is already going through hell; so it is a crucial time for you to be the most supportive, most nonjudgmental listener you can possibly be. Any "why didn't you . . .?" or "why were you . . .?" questions are only likely to reinforce a youngster's own despair and self-blame. Just listen and comfort and reinforce the truth that she was not to blame. *Whatever the circumstances*, rape is always a gross violation of the victim's basic human rights.

While continuing your unconditional support, immediately contact your local rape crisis center. Look under "Rape" in the telephone directory or dial the operator for the hotline number. These centers have an outstanding track record for providing round-the-clock assistance, support, and medical and legal information. A trained worker will help your youngster, and you, through the next few critical hours and the days ahead. Calling a rape center does not mean that the rape must be reported to the police. All rape hotline calls are confidential, and you can even remain anonymous, if you wish to.

Preserve the evidence. The youngster should not shower or

bathe or douche, and the clothes should be gathered in bags (one for each item) if she changes. It is important that the evidence (hair, blood, saliva, semen) not be washed away.

Get her examined medically and have any needed treatment performed. Go with her to the hospital or doctor's office and stay with her through the exam if she wants you to. The possibility of pregnancy or sexually transmitted disease from the rapist needs to be handled, whether formal charges are filed or not. The local rape center probably can provide someone to go along to the hospital if further support is needed. (Don't neglect the fact that *you* may need this support.)

Follow these same procedures if the victim is male.

Parents of teenage rape victims understandably may want to press charges. But Robin Warshaw and other rape experts strongly recommend letting the youngster make the decisions on how to proceed. As Warshaw points out: "Try to separate how you feel about what has happened from what is best for the [youngster's] recovery. If she decides not to report it, and you disagree with that, let her know that you support her decision nonetheless."

Getting a conviction for date rape is often difficult. This is especially true if the couple had been drinking or using drugs together in a private place or if there was much of a prior relationship between them. A trial so often boils down to his story against hers, which raises too much "reasonable doubt" to bring in a guilty verdict. And the victim, already distraught, usually finds the judicial system traumatic in itself. However, filing a police report, even if charges aren't pressed, will give the culprit some trauma too, and the report will remain on his record. Much judicial reform is *still* badly needed in this area.

Continue your support in the following days, weeks, and months, whatever option the youngster chooses. Let her know you're available if she wants to talk. Get her psychological counseling if she wishes. Counseling may be available at school or the local women's center. She might also want to join a post-rape support group. Think "survivor," not "victim," and help the wounds heal.

Rape experts stress that the single biggest factor in alleviating the trauma of rape, speeding recovery, and getting on with life is *the unconditional support of family, friends, and rape crisis centers*.

#66

Dealing with Drugs

Somebody once wrote: "The world abounds with laws and teems with crime," and this surely seems the case sometimes as parents strive to steer their youngsters safely through the teenage years. Of major concern is the drug abuse epidemic. This concern is justified, yet there is good news too. Recently drug abuse has declined steadily year after year among almost all segments of the teenage population. And these rate decreases apply to all types of illicit drugs.

Why the declines? Evidently they are not due to drug enforcement. Despite the often-heroic efforts of law officers, drug supplies remain plentiful almost everywhere. The main reason seems to be the launching and maintaining of intensive drug education programs at the national and local levels, often carried out by ex-users who know the score. Another helpful factor is that teenagers themselves have been seeing what sorry messes heavy abusers make of their lives. Happily, the general teenage culture is becoming more antidrug.

In no way is it true that youngsters who experiment with illegal drugs are tainted for life. Yet it is true that drugs are very unpredictable and every bit as dangerous as we've been told they are.

You might wonder why kids use illicit drugs anyway. One main reason is peer pressure. Surveys show that youngsters virtually always first try drugs in the company of users.

The other main reason is that drugs work—they *are* mood-altering substances. Kids use drugs for the same reasons that adults offer guests a drink, include wine as part of a romantic interlude, or get prescription pills from their doctors for physical and emotional pain. In copying adult society, however, teens usually have far too little regard for the horrendous possible side effects, dangers, and consequences of what they are doing.

The youth drug scene exists out of sight from most adults. It is a subculture of impulsive behaviors, restless unfocused rebellion, secretiveness, promiscuity, and illicit delinquent activities, such as robbing and shoplifting. Street dealers are usually other teens, in it for the money or to secure their own supplies. In the shadows, at the wholesale level, are some really ugly, violent characters. Kids who experiment with drugs are flirting with this world. It is not a happy world; kids on drugs are three times as likely to attempt suicide.

Experts have identified three distinct levels of teen drug abuse: The first is experimentation, usually resulting from curiosity, thrill-seeking, or peer pressure. The good news is that the majority of teens stop after one or a few scattered episodes. Regular use, where drugs are used for mood control and feeling good, is the second level. This is recreational use. The teen is still more or less in control and can easily stop. Sharply distinguished from these two levels is dependency/addiction. Acquiring drugs and maintaining a drugged state becomes all a person cares about. Addicts have lost control of their drug use; they will steal from parents, trade sex for drugs, or take up dealing drugs to maintain their supply. Most other teens stay away from addicts, who come to associate more and more exclusively with other steady users.

This third level of dependency/addiction should be regarded as what it is—a life-threatening illness—and some treatment is a virtual must. According to recovered addicts, physically kicking a dependency habit is much like going through a bad case of flu; the psychological dependency is the hard part to get over. This is why relapses are so common and why support groups, such as twelve-step programs, can be so important. The best treatment is, of course, never starting or at least stopping use at an earlier stage.

Complicated issues surround drug use; for instance, we still don't know to what extent there is a genetic predisposition to dependency/addiction. Yet there is much parents can do to thwart possible abuse.

- Nonusing teens must be alert to possible victimization from users. Users are prone to date rape and assault, to stealing from other teens, and to perpetrating violence that nonusers can get caught up in accidentally. There are two main safeguards for these risks. First, teens should avoid contact with users—they shouldn't banter with them, go to parties they attend, loiter or hang out near them, or reply to their enticements beyond politely saying no and leaving. Second, following all the guidelines from previous sections of this book—at school, on the street, and at home—will provide teens strong protection.
- When your kids are still little, firmly communicate your opposition to drug use. Let your kids know what a bummer drugs can be, without being a goodie-two-shoes about it. Facts have proven more effective than preaching. The earlier you start this, the better.
- Learn something about drugs and the youth drug scene. You'll want to know more than the little pamphlets tell you. Check with the school counselor or your local librarian; there are many good books available. An excellent book that addresses knowingly the details of substance abuse, sex, and parent-child communication is Ruth Bell and Leni Wildflower's *Talking with Your Teenager*. We also strongly recommend York, York, and Wachtel's *ToughLove* to parents facing unruly teens. Robert Schwebel's *Saying No Is Not Enough* is also good. You can receive a free copy of the Department of Education's excellent handbook, *Growing Up Drug Free: A Parent's Guide to Prevention*, simply by calling 1 800 624–0100.

■ Whatever is transpiring with your own job and personal life, strive to keep in touch, and use your interpersonal bridge to steer your youngster toward nonuser associates and activities. This is sometimes tough to do and it may not work, but conversations with nonusers show that it often does. According to National PTA president Ann Lynch, research indicates that actions taken by parents are the most influential factors in keeping children drug free.

■ The common signs of *possible* drug use are a sudden increase in secretiveness and withdrawal from family interactions, a drop of interest in previously pursued activities, a shift in associates and schedules, a plunge in school performance, and increased hostility and uncooperativeness. These could signal other things, such as sexual involvement, depression, a romantic breakup, or just passing moodiness. But something is up and deserves checking out.

■ If you discover your kids are using drugs, don't let it slide—intervene. It's not the end of the world, nor the end of your child, but it needs to be taken seriously. Talk with them about it as calmly as you can; candidly communicate your disapproval, feelings, and fears; and try to get an agreement on some ground rules. Talk with someone, such as a school counselor, who is experienced in youthful drug abuse. But if he or she has a "poor misunderstood kid; what have you rotten parents done wrong?" attitude, walk out and find somebody else. Parent-bashing is the last thing you need.

■ Make youngsters responsible for the consequences of their abuse. Many parents who've been through it say they made the mistake of covering for their kids, paying fines, and getting them off the hook. They said that this only prolonged the process and contributed indirectly to continuing the abuse.

■ If youngsters lose control and become dependent or addicted, there are no easy answers, but workers have learned a few hard-won lessons. Stay in communication and express love, but do not coddle addicts. Protect the rest of the family from falling into codependency; be aware that addicts will probably use deceitful and manipulative tactics to maintain their habit. You'll want to secure bank accounts, credit cards, trust funds, expensive jewelry, and so on, from them. (Not infrequently, they will burglarize their own homes.) Withdraw the family resources that are allowing them to exploit you. Offer treatment-recovery programs, but don't enforce them; no program will work unless the abuser is willing. Twelve-step programs, such as Narcotics Anonymous and the teen division of Alcoholics Anonymous, are very successful, and they ask only for small donations.

■ Get help for yourself, at least supportive friends from your parents' network. Drug-abusing children are bound to be emotionally distressing; don't bottle it up. The better shape you are in, the more help you are likely to be to the youngsters, yourself, and everyone else involved.

■ Have heart—time is probably on your side. Most regular users, and even addicts, grow out of abuse as they mature into young adulthood, are out on their own with bills to pay, a job, and perhaps a family of their own. Most "come to their senses" by their early twenties.

#67

Curbing Teen Drinking

Most parents would much rather have their kids use alcohol than drugs, and the kids have gotten the message—most kids *do* use alcohol instead of drugs. In fact, alcohol is the intoxicant of choice among the vast majority of teenagers.

Parents, police, and school authorities are usually much less concerned by a youngster's underage drinking than by illicit drug use, but experienced substance-abuse counselors can tell you how foolish this is.

One big problem with alcohol doesn't exist with illicit drugs. Not only is liquor legal in our society, it also gets promoted heavily by the best advertising agencies serving giant corporations with a great deal of political clout. In countless powerful ad images, beer is linked with sports and conviviality, wine is linked with romance and relaxation. Kids grow up with this constant promotional background. You don't offer heroin to a guest, but how about a drink?

Alcohol has been used in the majority of serious crimes and accidents involving teenagers—rape, assaults, homicides, vandalism, and serious auto accidents. Even if a youngster drinks little or nothing, drunken companions are dangerous. Precise physiological studies have documented the fact that even one drink measurably lowers perceptual discernment and reflexes. (One drink triples the odds of being in an accident.) And possible alcohol addiction is also a threat.

The guidelines for avoiding underage drinking problems are similar in most respects to those for drug abuse discussed in the last section. Yet there are important differences to keep in mind. Our whole society is more liquor-friendly than drug-friendly. You yourself may be more ambivalent about liquor and less firm in your opposition to your kids using it. Your own drinking can make liquor attractive and acceptable. Also, although teenager culture is becoming increasingly antidrug, it remains largely supportive of drinking. *Most teenagers still drink,* at least occasionally. The other main difference is that parents and authorities unfortunately tend not to intervene until much later in teenagers' progression of alcohol use—until youngsters show signs of full-blown dependency or a really serious incident happens. All these pro-alcohol influences might seem formidable, but your own curbing influence still can make the difference.

Educating your children young, before a problem arises, works best. Preaching about "demon drink" doesn't work very well. The best approach is to give kids factual data on the effects of alcohol and the risk of addiction. You can get these facts from your local library or school district.

Encourage and support local community and school alcohol education programs. Because so many teens and grown-ups think underage drinking is no big deal, they need to come to the realization that it *is* a big deal.

If your kids come home intoxicated or smelling of liquor, don't be too upset—chances that they will are excellent. Firmly communicate your disapproval without destroying your interpersonal bridge with them. Also, tailor your family rules, such as curfews and driving privileges, to curtail alcohol use.

Because alcohol and driving are one of the most dangerous mixes, establish the agreement that you will pick up your youngsters or pay for a cab, anywhere, whatever the circumstances. Many communities have found that such agreements do cut down on drunken teenage driving.

As with drugs, don't ignore or deny signs that your children have a drinking problem. If there's any progression from occasional tippling to steady, regular use, it's time to intervene in a big way. Confer with an experienced youth substance-abuse counselor, and with other parents who have been in a similar situation, to work out a game plan. Keep your love and communication flowing, but don't coddle or cover for the kids. The first step in recovery is for them to realize that they have a real problem.

Strive to get abusing youngsters into some kind of treatment program as soon as possible. They will have to make at least a halfhearted agreement to participate. Some of the best programs are support groups composed of other teen problem-drinkers, usually mediated by a trained counselor who is often a recovered substance abuser. Local schools may have such a program; also the teen division of Alcoholics Anonymous has an excellent record. Fellow users have many advantages as a support group. They have been there, they know how it happens, they can't be conned or manipulated very easily, and they provide a safe place for extremely candid communications. You, or even an experienced counselor, can be fooled far more easily than these fellow-traveling peers can.

And again, get some support yourself, to keep your own head and heart straight.

#68

Party Advisories

Teenage parties are one of the most likely places where your children can become involved in illegal activities—drugs, underage drinking, driving while intoxicated, rowdiness, and other actions that come to the unfavorable attention of the police. They can also lead to victimizations, such as acquaintance rape or aggravated assault. So they deserve some special attention. Even when the party starts out innocently, the "group high" and party crashers sometimes cause it to get out of control as the hours go by. To youngsters, a party is an adventure and, short of locking them in their rooms, you probably can't keep them away. What you *can* do is try for some commonsense curbs.

Never allow a party in your home when you are not there, and discourage your kids from going to unsupervised parties at other homes. If your kids have parties at your dwelling, don't disappear discreetly. Actively supervise them. Call and ask the parents of your youngsters' friends to do the same. You might be accused of not being cool, but who cares? Your priority is your children's security.

Don't serve or allow alcohol at your youngsters' party and ask their friends' parents to do the same. Adults can't control entirely what goes on during youthful bashes, even in their own homes. Enforced curfews help you maintain some control. Even when they are not quite followed, they keep your parental presence alive in the youngsters' mind. You have influence—use it.

Have the understanding that you will come get your kids or pay for a cab, wherever they are, "no questions asked," if they do get intoxicated or run into trouble.

Unless it would involve personal danger, let them take the rap for any consequences of their party-going, such as a fine or driver's license suspension. Having to pay for some damages or losing one's license for a month can have nitty-gritty educational value.

#69

Morbid Moods

Giant mood swings seem to go hand in hand with being an adolescent. These swings result partly from the swift parade of hormonal changes and partly from the outcomes of teens' interpersonal adventures and misadventures. Kids can be on top of the world one hour and at the bottom of the cosmos the next, then bounce back again to sheepish good humor.

The problem arises when morbid moods persist, because they can predispose youngsters to negligence and extreme behavior. They are then more prone to being victimized or getting into criminality themselves. Unhappy youngsters are a vulnerable, high-risk group.

Glumness and withdrawal that persist might also signal a deep-running problem, such as drug use, pregnancy, a date rape, or a sexual incident, where the teens really need your help.

The signs of such a situation are usually easily seen—a real drop in communication with the rest of the family, loss of interest in activities the youths were formerly enthusiastic about, introverted withdrawal, and secretiveness. These signals should be taken seriously, and there are several things you can do.

The first thing is to "get in touch" by communicating. Engage youngsters in conversation; it doesn't matter what on. This reinforces your interpersonal bridge and will, all by itself, sometimes brings any lurking situation into the open.

If this doesn't work, candidly say you are concerned, and ask (don't demand), "What's up?" Let them know you are there for them, whatever is going on, and mean it.

You don't have to go it alone. By now your parents' network has probably turned into something of a support group. Use it to talk out your own feelings and concerns. You'll be better able to cope, whatever the situation turns out to be, and other parents might have some answers from their own hard-won experiences.

Also, discourage or don't even allow upset youngsters to go out on their own. People who are emotionally distressed or angry are far more vulnerable to becoming crime victims. Such a misfortune is not inevitable, but the odds have shifted in the wrong direction. People who are distraught tend to be more careless and reckless than they usually are. They are less alert, less rational, and more likely to take "who-cares" and "what-the-hell" stupid chances.

Reports amply show that when youngsters (or anyone) feel rotten, they often will try drugs, drink more than usual, pick a fight, have a sexual fling, or stalk off down a dark street by themselves. People in recovery programs sometimes relapse at such times.

It is best if children learn about the risks accompanying emotional upsets early on, *before* adolescence. If you are going through a divorce, have lost a job, or have been forced to move, your kids are likely to be more emotionally distressed, upset, and vulnerable. Point this out to them.

If your upset youngsters want to go out, your taking them somewhere would combine companionship and supervision for them.

Train your youngsters that, if they become upset while they are out on their own, keeping enough presence of mind to get themselves home safely is their immediate priority.

If teenagers' morbid moods persist and home remedies aren't really working, get some outside help. You might start by talking with a school counselor. See if there is a local teen support group. You might also find and give your children the number of a teen hotline where they can talk things out confidentially with trained volunteers—often older teens who are in the know because they've been there. One such national hotline is 1 800 FOUR–KID.

#70

Avoiding Assault and Murder

According to the U.S. Department of Justice's National Crime Survey report, "average" violent crime victimization rates are more than twice as high for youths aged twelve to nineteen than for the rest of the population. Most incidents happened in high-crime locales, were gang- or drug-related, and involved gross violations of our seven mega-strategies. Your youngsters needn't be among these statistics. The two key strategies for your children to learn to apply for avoiding aggravated assault and murder are *Mega-Strategy Five: "Pick Your Spots,"* and *Mega-Strategy Seven: "Get Along."*

Picking your spots is so important because most violent crimes occur at certain times and places. Being on the streets or at a teen hangout in a high-crime zone late at night, for example, doubles all risk factors.

Getting along is equally important because most of these incidents involve a "partnership" in aggressiveness, as studies such as the one by criminologists Richard Felson and Henry Steadman show. In many cases the victim was even the one who started it—by smart remarks, antagonizing gestures, or showing a weapon.

In avoiding violent crime, interpersonal factors are as important as closing and locking. Although bystanders occasionally get caught up in "random" violence, investigators have found that there is usually some sort of victim participation in assaults and homicides. Even a youngster's idle conversational style can be companionable or provoking.

The secret of getting along is good manners. Your kids must

learn to say no as we've seen, but it can be done politely, without any added rancor or putdowns. Youngsters who make jokes at others' expense, who chronically gossip, or who bad-mouth someone they broke up with are making enemies who may choose their own retaliations. Train your children to walk on by if they are taunted or verbally insulted. You don't know what kind of person, under what influence, you might be dealing with.

Boys have more problems avoiding these dances of anger than girls because of the lingering macho stereotypes that males are still pushed to live up to. Our society retains something of a love affair with the warrior. Raising boys to be "tough guys" and girls to be "nice girls" is a real disservice to everyone. These old stereotypes push male kids toward aggressiveness and girls toward submissive vulnerability, codependencies, and the other ills the women's movement rightfully protests.

Another solution that many parents have found effective is to enroll their kids in martial arts or self-defense courses that have a nonviolent philosophy. These courses build youngsters' inner self-confidence and physical and emotional balance. Because of their increased self-control and poised body language, the graduates find that they are much less inviting to troublemakers.

The other major risk factor in assaults, criminal injuries, and homicides is youngsters' own illicit or reckless life-style. Life-styles that involve gang membership, drugs, gay cruising, hustling, or running away from home are many times more prone to violent victimization. *The most common victims of youthful criminals are other youths who are also engaged in illegalities.* And in 70 percent of cases, the violence occurs while the youths are under the influence of drugs or alcohol.

A lot of people survive such life-styles, but some don't. In careful investigations over many years, the former Chief Joe McNamara, of the San Jose Police Department, has found there is usually some crimeprone life-style component, even in the homicide victimizations of seemingly innocent people. He reports that in a great many cases the public never learns about all the facts.

Steer your youngsters away from the beginnings of any such life-style and you'll be enhancing their survival in many ways.

#71

Securing Money and Valuables

The earlier youngsters learn to protect their money and valuables, the better, because they will need this savvy throughout their lives. The teen years can serve as a valuable money-handling "apprenticeship." Crime experts have worked out a series of straightforward guidelines that you can teach your kids verbally and by your own good example.

■ Don't carry more cash than you can afford to lose.

■ Get your youngsters into the habit of carrying a bit of emergency cash in another pocket or somewhere else about their person. Some enterprising parents sew a little pocket somewhere inside their youngsters' clothes in which to keep phone money.

■ Teach your kids to hide away their excess cash from potential burglaries. Burglars are almost always in a rush and only have time to ransack obvious places in a dwelling. Money put in an old dictionary, in the back of a hanging picture, or inside a scruffy stuffed toy will almost certainly be missed. Many families keep a communal emergency cash fund creatively hidden away.

■ Youngsters, especially boys, are susceptible to "petty" muggings. The risks of this are greatly reduced if they travel with other kids and stay in public view. Boys who are mugged are likely to feel humiliated, yet they need realistic data, not "real men give karate chops." It is important that they follow the "on the spot" recommendations from Strategy 37: surrender their valuables without any argument, resistance, or unnecessary dialogue, and get the episode over with as quickly as possible. (The average mugging lasts ninety seconds.)

Some parents have adopted the clever idea of providing their youngsters with "mugger money"—an old wallet with a couple dollars in it. Wearing cheaper watches and costume jewelry, rather than expensive items or family heirlooms, is also a good idea because stealing and mugging are fairly common, especially in the early teen years.

■ Managing money with security and good sense is something most of us are still learning about. It is very helpful for growing youths to begin learning the ins and outs of these things with modest amounts of money—to practice when there's less to lose. Arrange for youngsters to have their own bank accounts and, when older, a joint credit card; bank and credit card transactions are far more secure than using much cash. They might get credit card fever and charge to the limit, then wrestle with having to pay it off. Many of us have had to go through such an experience at least once. Aside from foolish spending, youngsters need to know a few fundamentals. First, be wary of giving out credit card numbers and never give them to unknown persons unless you initiate the transaction. Second, don't use automatic teller machines in isolated spots or during off-hours, and never late at night. It is not a good idea to use your birth date as your PIN (Personal Identification Number). Crooks know that most people do this; use a famous date or some easily remembered personal milestone date instead. Third, always take special precautions in depositing, withdrawing, or carrying any large sums of cash. Criminals have shown almost uncanny ingenuity in ferreting out such transactions. Finally, alertly follow all prevention tips and don't hesitate to ask for escort help from security personnel.

If your teen has a lot of valuable items, such as stereo equipment and computer systems, inventory them and purchase an inexpensive insurance rider on your own home policy. This is especially wise if your household is a "sociable" one with lots of people streaming in and out.

#72

Avoiding Scams

Most scams and con games target adults and senior citizens because that's where the real money is. However, teenagers with their discretionary dollars are not immune, and they need to learn the art of scam-dodging anyway. The following pointers are drawn from Federal Trade Commission recommendations and State Attorney General advisories.

■ While 800 phone numbers are free, the caller pays varying rates by the minute for all 900 numbers. These latter should always be regarded warily. Youngsters may be enticed into calling them on many pretexts—a rock-star idol, telephone sex, fabulous money-making offers, psychic readings, what have you. What you as a parent get is a whopping phone bill. The easiest tactic is to forbid any 900 number calling without your explicit permission. You might also make the agreement that children pay for all their own calls.

■ If any offer seems too good to be true, it almost certainly is. Con artists prey upon two basic human emotions, greed and fear. No stranger is likely to freely give away fabulous prizes or trips. And no service is likely to magically transform your youngster.

■ Don't impulse buy. Always check out a company's track record with other adults, the Better Business Bureau, *Consumer Reports*, or a trusted family advisor. Many mail-order companies offer excellent prices and service on items teenagers buy, such as stereo equipment and CDs, but some are total frauds.

■ There is a large gray area of shoddy semiscams. While

they are within the limits of the law, you don't get your money's worth. There are fad products, unreliable used-car dealerships, overpriced waterbeds, jeans, or shoes where you pay double just for the label, and so on. Heavy advertising hype and high-pressure salesmanship are the trademarks of such semiscams, so help your children to resist them. Keep in mind, though, that what may appear a scam to you, like owl-frame glasses or a heavy-metal band CD, may not be to them.

#73

Part-time Job Security

Part-time jobs give your teenagers work experience and the blessings of their own money. All the tactics we've covered previously will do much to protect fledgling workers from crime, but there are some valuable additional pointers.

Check the job situation out before giving your approval. Is it in a relatively safe locale? Are the employers reputable? Is the location sufficiently safe? In your investigation, keep in mind that times have changed. For instance, a few decades ago, a paper route was a good job for a bike-riding youngster, but now such a job is iffy. These days, you would also want to know just whom your teen is baby-sitting for before saying okay. Your parent and neighborhood networks can be excellent resources for both information and good job leads.

Without nagging, firmly check with your youngsters that they are routinely following security guidelines, such as staying public while on the job and when entering or leaving. Encourage them to adopt a "buddy system" if they are working in a public establishment so they don't go to and from their transportation alone. Also give them "booster" reminders about elevators, back stairs, deserted sections of buildings, and listening to their gut feelings. Part of the charm of adolescents is their exuberance and zest, but this can also lead them into being careless.

Virtually every job location will have at least some sort of rudimentary security system. Ask your children about it and insist that they learn it. Include the fire alarm system, because this can be commandeered for personal security. Yelling "Fire" and tripping an alarm often brings more help than anything else. If your teens handle money or go into secluded areas as part of the job, insist that they are always accompanied at least by another employee, preferably by security.

If your teens are supposed to work off-hours, especially late at night when there are few people around, insist that there is adequate security.

If you have questions about the on-the-job security, don't hesitate to make your own inquiries. And if you really have a bad feeling about the job situation, help your youngsters find other employment.

Let your children know that the workplace is a prime place for petty, and not so petty, theft. Valuables and purses need to be watched or secured even when teens just run out to the restroom or for a drink of water. Workplace thieves are usually extremely swift and nimble. The same care should be taken on baby-sitting jobs, because smaller kids will sometimes snatch money or small valuables, even if just for the thrill.

Your teens should know some facts about getting along with others on the job when they start to work outside the home. The simple fact, clearly shown by psychological research, is that people tend to help and protect those they like, while they are indifferent, if not spiteful, toward the fate of those they don't.

If someone backbites, puts down, unfairly competes with, belittles, or otherwise needlessly antagonizes the other people connected with a job, those on the receiving end are likely to take it *very* personally. They are likely to harbor ill will and cause mischief sooner or later, in one way or another. Aside from making the workplace more tense and unpleasant, this accumulated ill will can burst forth in retaliations ranging from petty vandalism to homicide.

Getting along has nothing to do with being a pushover. Nor does one have to be Mother Teresa. Good manners, a considerate attitude, and a mild display of fellowship with others will do the trick. Friendly coworkers, bosses, and customers are a bulwark against crime; unfriendly ones can be a source of it.

Incidentally, you might want to double-check your own on-the-job security habits so your kids are not victimized by *your* running into trouble.

#74

Dealing with Gangs

Parents are justifiably concerned that their kids might be victimized by delinquent gangs or be influenced to join them. A great deal of youthful crime is, in fact, gang related. Law enforcement agencies have struggled with gangs for decades now with only modest success. In Brazil the problem has gotten so bad that local merchants and citizens often hire private hit squads simply to kill young criminals.

You can study long without finding any easy answers to the causes or cures of delinquent gangs. But we do know *some* things. First, don't confuse rowdiness and misbehavior with full-blown gang activity. Teens habitually form cliques that may play around with underage drinking, "tasting" drugs, and petty vandalism. However, true gang activity goes far beyond these things; it involves drug dealing, car thefts, and burglaries, carrying lethal weapons, assaults, turf wars—in other words, really serious criminality.

Second, *your teens don't have to join a gang*. Even in gang-infested areas, most youths are not gang members. Gangs don't pressure everyone to join. They are often quite selective; aspirants have to apply and prove themselves through criminal acts. "Pressures to join" are mostly internal; that is, youths are personally attracted to the gang life-style.

Why do youths join gangs? Members give these answers: a sense of belonging and camaraderie with fellow members; thrills and adventures to spark up an otherwise bleak life; the prestige and power of being a recognized member—empowerment; the profit motive—abundant money, desired goods, and easily available sex. Membership is further justified by pointing to the hypocrisy of straight society ("Look at the S & L bandits, man") and the mess the world is in ("I'll be dead by the time I'm twenty").

So what should a parent do?

■ If gangs are active in your locale or school, it is imperative to redouble the security training of your kids—home security and street smarts and Strategy 38, "Surviving Street Violence."

■ Even before your children reach puberty, clearly communicate your opposition to the gang life-style. Look for realistic antigang documentaries and view them with your children.

■ Steer your youngsters toward constructive activities and goals, such as science hobbies, sports, or scholastic achievement, so that gangland has less allure for them.

■ Exhort them to curtail contact with gang members and gang hangout spots. Be polite and refrain from verbal antagonisms, but stay aloof. Especially stay out of gang politics or rivalries.

■ If you find yourself in a gang-infested neighborhood, move if you can. Carefully follow the procedures given in Strategy 15, "Choosing Where to Live," in picking a new place.

■ If you can't move, redouble efforts to build a strong anticrime neighborhood network. Even in the most crime-ridden locales, most of the inhabitants are law abiding and interested in security. In liaison with the local police, the network can also implement plans to "take back the neighborhood," which many locales have done successfully. Together with other parents, also pressure school officials to "take back the school" if it has become gang ridden.

■ If your children become involved with a gang, try to keep communication open and your interpersonal bridge in place. But don't cover for them or be tolerant of their illegalities.

(Many delinquents straighten out after one brush with the law, especially if there are alternative programs to steer them into. In fact, around nine out of ten youthful offenders leave gang behavior behind when they leave adolescence and move into young adulthood.)

#75

Preventing Runaways

Establishing a strong interpersonal bridge with love and open communication early on and maintaining it as children grow are the most effective strategies against ever having to face a runaway situation. So, by strongly keeping in touch, you are taking effective preventive action even when children are still toddlers.

Some children run away because of an intolerable home scene—chronic physical, sexual, or emotional abuse. A minority of them are actually "throwaways" whose parents have abandoned them. In most cases running away is a highly emotional, impulsive response to situations, such as a bitter argument over rules and expectations, where youngsters see no alternatives.

Most runaways don't go very far and return home within a couple of days, but if this occurs, it is a signal to be taken very seriously. Threats to run away are also messages that should not be ignored.

Often children enter adolescence, with all its changes and challenges, at the same time the parents are at the height of career pressures and goals. This double situation can lead too easily to unintentional neglect and an interpersonal breakdown. "Little lambie-pie" becomes a sometimes surly, sometimes defiant semistranger, experimenting with who knows what, while work demands seem to endlessly encroach on your time and patience. In scenarios like this, misunderstandings can grow quickly and tempers can flare beyond control. Even when the parent-child relationship becomes this tense, there's much a parent can do to stop it from becoming a runaway scene.

Sit down with your children and talk it out together. Be a good listener, but also communicate your own views and pressures, without giving more details than they can handle. So often kids don't have much understanding of what a *parent* is going through. Above all, let them know you care. Even joking about running away is usually a veiled plea that youngsters feel trapped, neglected, or misunderstood. If you feel the same way, let them know, and seek solutions together.

If you need to go back to school for an advanced degree or put in extra work while starting up a new business, talk it over with the kids beforehand. Discuss the eventual benefits as well as the present travails, so they understand why you are doing it.

Somewhere along the line it would also be good if the kids learned about the stark realities of street life for young runaways—the privations, dangers, and frequent victimizations. Keep your eye out for a good TV documentary or magazine article covering these harsh realities and share it with them. Too often children don't realize what they'd likely be running *to*.

If teens threaten to run off, and talking it out doesn't go very well, consider getting a third person both of you trust as an arbiter. This often helps to sidestep any entrenched defensive patterns a parent and child have built up, such as disagreements over companions or curfews. Some parents have arranged a safe place for a teen to run to, such as the home of a grandparent or family friend. You can also supply youngsters with local and national teen hotline numbers, where they can talk with other teens who are likely to be supportive and understanding of whatever they are going through.

Whatever happens with your teens, remember that you are far from totally responsible for their choices and their lives. There are many well-documented cases of kids who come from an indifferent, authoritarian, or even abusive family and yet go on to establish a successful productive life. Conversely, there are many authentic reports of kids coming from a loving, supportive family of opportunity who nevertheless take up a sleazy street life. Kids are *persons* in their own right, who make (or don't make) their own bed, call their own shots, and do their own sowing and reaping.

#76

Dodging Cults

A fairly common fear among parents is that their youthful offspring will be lost to a cult. The good news is that cults have been shrinking rapidly in both influence and numbers in recent years, so there is much less risk of this happening than there was a decade ago. But some precautions are still in order. The following data are drawn from anticult groups, such as the American Family Foundation, and from the authors' interviews with former cult members.

What distinguishes a cult from ordinary groups and organizations? Sometimes "cult" is just a term thrown at some outfit the accuser doesn't like. And sometimes parents fear that a youngster's fierce infatuation with some celebrity, such as Madonna, has cult overtones. But true cults have two distinguishing marks. The first is an obsessive involvement on the part of members. The second is exclusiveness and separateness from the rest of society. Cults can be strictly local or international in size. They can espouse vaulting, lofty causes, claiming to be the True Way to personal and global transformations, although their tenets might sound crazy to nonmembers. Occasionally cults become major social movements or even new major religions. Virtually any cult does contain at least some bits and pieces of truth. But in our time, cults have usually proven to be emotionally harmful, disruptive to families, and a financial ripoff.

Contemplating strange new notions is one thing—after all, today's outlandish idea has, again and again, turned out to be tomorrow's proven fact. But getting embroiled in a cult is quite something else. Cults provide people with two things they want: a passionate Cause that gives their life meaning, and a strong sense of fellowship and belonging with other members and the group. Cults rely upon intense psychological persuasion and emotional manipulation. These Pied Piper tactics lead the members to share an exalted in-group conviction that they are THE WAY (and the only Way).

Whether it is a local Satanic group or an international "church," cults capture the minds, hearts, loyalties, and finances of their members. Through what usually amounts to brainwashing techniques, newcomers are turned into unquestioning, lockstep adherents. How far off the rails a cult can go is shown by the tragic Jonestown incident, where some 900 people committed "suicide" together in Guyana, and the doings of some Satanic groups that have recently come to light.

But the vast majority of members eventually do escape a cult's clutches. Ex-members describe the life inside cults as very stringent and demanding. For the sake of the Cause, you are expected to sacrifice, often working sixteen hours a day, while you are cut off from the rest of the world. You are judged by your fervor—and questioning the leaders is tantamount to blasphemy.

Perhaps the most tragic aspect of cults is that they frequently tear families apart. Members are persistently exhorted to adopt the cult as their "true family." They are told either to bring the rest of their family into the fold or cut their ties. If other family members object to the cult's doings, they are denounced.

In appraising some group youngsters are interested in, there are three telltale danger signs to look for.

1. If the group exalts some human leader or founder to more-than-human status, it is almost certainly a cult. Admiration and affection toward exceptional persons is one thing; abject worship and unquestioning devotion is quite another.

2. If the group extracts large sums of money and unquestioning servitude from members, it is almost certainly a cult. Most worthy organizations charge only modest membership and service fees and do not preempt all your waking hours.

3. If the group contemptuously rejects all other groups, while claiming it is the only True Way, it is probably a cult.

Happily, only a tiny fraction of organizations are true cults. There are plenty of groups with admirable causes and warm fellowship among their members. In the legitimate ones, nobody claims to be a demigod and membership fees are a few dollars, not all your house and lands.

The come-ons to join a cult can be very sophisticated and persuasive. If your children are interested in some group that you have questions about, consider going with them to check it out. Two people are much harder to seduce into groupthink than one, and your presence will help prevent youngsters from being hypnotized.

Open parent-child communication, a warm supportive home environment, and meaningful activities within legitimate organizations are the greatest deterrent to cult involvement. The activities must, however, be meaningful from your youngsters' viewpoint.

If youngsters are still underage, you have legal recourse against their joining a cult, but this is tricky and may further alienate the children. If your children have joined a cult, the best thing is to contact one of the cult retrieval groups that are experienced in such matters for guidance, such as the American Family Foundation.

If youngsters do become involved, don't be argumentative. Stay in open communication as best you can, let them talk it out, and recognize that the vast majority of members *do* leave cults sooner or later.

Former cult members usually go through a period of disorientation and loss. Help them get going again, provide emotional and other needed support, and please refrain from saying "I told you so."

EPILOGUE

Leaving the Nest

Some anonymous sage once wrote that the end of anything is always the beginning of something else. So it is when your youngsters finally leave the family nest and set out on their own independent life. You will probably experience a complicated mixture of heartache and relief when this happens. The advice from psychologists is, don't repress the heartache and don't feel guilty about the sense of relief.

Whether your youngsters are going off to college, getting their own job and apartment, or getting married, they are doing something new—setting up their own independent housekeeping and daily life routine. This marks the beginning of their adulthood.

There will be a transition period, lasting several months or more, where fledgling adults return to being innocents abroad all over again. For instance, *everyone* always seems to underestimate just how much it costs to set up a household. A safe rule is probably to estimate the cost, then double the estimate.

While youngsters are living at home most of their money is discretionary, but after they move out, little of it may be. There are probably a hundred and one things, from your washer and dryer to your insurance coverage, that they took for granted while they lived at home. Now these many kinds of supports won't be there.

Often, neither the youths nor the parents realize the high level of security the family nest has been providing. It is taken for granted as background—until it isn't there. They now need somehow to get their own laundry done and their own bills paid. And their security from crime is almost completely in their own hands.

Well, you've spent the last couple of decades preparing them for this, and now it's up to them.

When they first leave the roost, there's a tendency for youths to live it up a little or a lot. Keeping in touch (without butting in) will help dampen this tendency and will also help them and you through this psychological weaning process. A few phone calls and a spate of letters can do wonders, both for giving them emotional support and for keeping your family's values alive in their minds and hearts. If they feel abandoned abruptly, they are more likely to stray in dangerous directions.

When youths move out from the family home, it is a milestone in the lives of all those involved. It heralds a qualitative change in the parent-child relationship. No, things will never be the same. But there is the opportunity to form a new kind of relationship and companionship. Never lose sight of *Mega-Strategy One*, *"Keep in Touch."*

Your youngsters will continue to carry all your security training inside themselves. And despite your fumbling, and their fumbling, most kids turn out just fine.

APPENDIX

Where to Get Help

We have shown throughout this book that there is actually a tremendous amount of help available for parents and their children. Support groups, hotlines, and public and private nonprofit agencies are ready to give aid in almost every conceivable sort of parent-child situation. Just knowing there are other people out there who care can be reassuring.

There are two main reasons why these resources are not even more widely used. First, many people don't know about them or how to reach them. Second, some people hesitate to use them. Don't hesitate—reach out; people are waiting to help you on the other end of the phone or mail line. Helping is the sole reason for these groups' existence.

A caution: Some for-profit clinics and other organizations now have hotlines or emergency numbers, but they use them to promote their own, often very expensive, services. If you run into this, just politely end the communication and look elsewhere. Most help organizations are free or ask only for very modest donations to cover expenses.

Also, we have taken pains to gather together a list that is both current and reliable. But times change, so we cannot guarantee the continuing accuracy or ethics of the entries.

Responsibility for contacting them and any subsequent interactions rest solely with the reader.

A great many hotlines and help groups are either local or statewide, so we are unable to list these. More and more local phone directories now list area hotlines and emergency numbers in the first few pages of the book. The national organizations listed in this section also usually can supply local referrals. When writing national organizations, enclose a self-addressed stamped business envelope.

It is a wise move to collect "Help" names, phone numbers, and addresses in a minidirectory of your own. This is also something your network can do together, sharing the numbers and photocopying lists and updates. It is hoped that you will never need them. But you might run into someone else—a coworker or acquaintance or relative—who does. They are awfully nice to have handy.

Emergency Numbers

Have emergency numbers permanently posted by each of your phones. These should minimally include Police, Fire, Paramedic/Ambulance, and relatives and friends you can count on. In emergencies people sometimes can't recall even simple numbers, so have them handy at all times. Around the country "911" is fast becoming a standard emergency number, but check to see that it is in your area. If you don't know what else to do, dial "O" for Operator.

Local and Statewide Listings

Most local and statewide listings will be in the white pages of your phone book or in the special section of government office listings. National organizations, such as Alcoholics Anonymous or the (McGruff) National Crime Prevention Council, very often have local chapters listed in your white pages. Or you can contact the national headquarters listed in the next section.

At a minimum, it is wise to gather and have at hand the following local and state phone numbers and addresses:

- Alcoholics Anonymous
- Ambulance/paramedics
- Attorney General (state)
- Auto club
- Better Business Bureau
- Consumer Protection Agency
- Credit card consumer hotlines
- Crime Prevention Unit (Local police—business number)
- District Attorney's Office
- Family doctor(s)
- FBI
- Fire Department (emergency and business office)
- Friends of the family (reliable)
- Highway Patrol
- Insurance agents
- Police (emergency and business office)
- Rape crisis hotline or rape center
- Relatives (reliable)
- School
- Social welfare agency hotline (local or state, may be listed under "Family Services" or "Child Welfare")
- United Way (referrals to appropriate local agencies)
- Women's Center

National Organizations

AIDS

National AIDS Hotline 1 800 342-AIDS.

ALCOHOL PROBLEMS

Al Anon (for relatives and friends of persons with alcohol problems) 1372 Broadway, New York, NY 10018. (212) 302-7240.

Al TEEN (for teens) 1372 Broadway, New York, NY 10018. (212) 302-7240.

Alcoholics Anonymous. Box 459, Grand Central Station, New York, NY 10163. (212) 686-1100. Local white pages.

National Clearinghouse for Alcohol Information. Box 2345, Rockville, MD 20852.

ANOREXIA

Anorexia/Bulimia Self-Help 1 800 BASH-STL.

National Association of Anorexia Nervosa. Box 7, Highland Park, IL 60035. (312) 831-3438.

ANTIGANG PROGRAMS

Boys and Girls Clubs of America. Local white pages. National, Dept. PM, 711 First Avenue, New York, NY 10017. (212) 351-5911

CHILD ABUSE

National Child Abuse Hotline 1 800 422-4453.

Parent's Anonymous Hotline 1 800 421-0353.

Parent's Anonymous (for parents who have abused their children). 6733 South Sepulveda Boulevard, Suite 270, Los Angeles, CA 90045. (213) 410-9732.

CHILDREN OUT OF CONTROL

ToughLove. Box 1069, Doylestown, PA 18901. 1 800 333-1069.

CODEPENDENCY

Co-Dependent Anonymous. Box 33577, Phoenix, AZ 85067.

CRIME PREVENTION

National Crime Prevention Council. 1700 K Street, Washington, D.C. 20006. (202) 466-6272.

DEPRESSION

Depressives Anonymous. 329 East 67th Street, New York, NY 10021 (include SASE). (212) 689-2600.

DOMESTIC VIOLENCE

National Coalition Against Domestic Violence (shelters and support services for battered women and their children). Box 15127, Washington, DC 20003-0127. Hotline 1 800 333-SAFE.

DRUG ABUSE

Drug Abuse (how and where to get help). 24-hour Hotline 1 800 COCAINE.

Drug Abuse Hotline. 1 800 662-HELP.

Narcotics Anonymous. Box 99, Van Nuys, CA 91409. (818) 780-3951.

National Clearinghouse for Drug Abuse Information. P.O. Box 416, Kensington, MD 20795.

Parents for Drug-Free Youth 1 800 554-KIDS.

PRIDE (Parent's Resource Institute for Drug Education). Hotline 1 800 241-9746.

EMOTIONAL PROBLEMS

Emotions Anonymous (twelve-step program for persons with emotional problems). Box 4245, St. Paul, MN 55104. (612) 647-9712.

FRAUD

Federal Trade Commission (write). 6th St. and Pennsylvania Ave. NW, Washington, DC 20580.

INCEST

Survivors of Incest Anonymous. Box 21817, Baltimore, MD 21222.

KIDS IN TROUBLE

Information and local help sources, 9 to 5 EST Monday to Friday: 1 800 554-KIDS.

LATCHKEY

Phone Friend, confidential "warm line" for latchkey kids. Local listings.

MENTAL ILLNESS

National Alliance for the Mentally Ill. 2101 Wilson Boulevard, Suite 302, Arlington, VA 22201. (703) 524-7600.

MISSING CHILDREN

Missing Children Network Hotline 1 800 235-3535.

POSTPARTUM DEPRESSION

Depression After Delivery (for women experiencing postpartum depression). Box 1282, Morrisville, PA 19067. (215) 295-3994.

RUNAWAYS

Coventry (for runaways) 1 800 999-9999.

Missing Children Network 1 800 235-3200.

SAFE HOUSES AND SAFE TRUCKS

National McGruff House Network (info on McGruff House and McGruff Truck programs). 1879 South Main, Suite 180, Salt Lake City, UT 84115. (801) 486-8768.

SINGLE PARENTS

Single Parent Resource Center. 141 West 38th Street, New York, NY 10001. (212) 947-0221.

SUICIDE

National Adolescent Suicide Hotline 1 800 621-4000.

SUMMER CAMPS ACCREDITATION

American Camping Association Hotline 1 800 428-CAMP.

VICTIMIZATION

National Organization for Victim Assistance (NOVA). 1757 Park Road, Washington, DC 20010. (202) 232-6682.

National Victim Center (advocacy and support referrals). 307 West 7th Street, Suite 1001, Fort Worth, TX 76102. (817) 877-3355.

National Victims Resource Center. Box 6000-AJE, Rockville, MD 20850. (301) 251-5525.

Victim Services Hotline (immediate help). (212) 577-7777.

Selected Bibliography

Berg, Barbara J. "Good News For Mothers Who Work." Parents (October 1986): 103–108.

Conklin, John. *Criminology*, 2nd ed. New York: Wiley, 1986.

FBI Uniform Crime Reports. Washington, D.C.: U.S. Government Printing Office (published annually).

Felson, Richard, and Henry Steadman. "Situational Factors in Disputes Leading to Criminal Violence." *Criminology* 21 (February 1983): 59–74.

Gondolf, Edward. *Men Against Women*. Blue Ridge Summit, PA: Tab, 1989.

Goode, Erich. *Deviant Behavior*, 2nd ed. Englewood Cliffs, NJ: Prentice-Hall, 1984.

Goodman, Ellen. "The Turmoil of Teenage Sexuality." *Ms* (July 1983): 37–41.

Gordon, Sol, Ph.D. "What Kids Need to Know." *Psychology Today* (October 1986): 22–26.

Gottfredson, Michael, and Travis Hirschi. "Why We're Losing the War on Crime." *Washington Post*, September 10, 1989.

Hall, Barbara. *Playing It Safe*. Buffalo, NY: Firefly, 1990.

Hechinger, Grace. *How to Raise a Street Smart Child*. New York: Facts On File, 1984.

Henslin, James M. *Social Problems*, 2nd ed. Englewood Cliffs, NJ: Prentice-Hall, 1990.

Hirschi, Travis, and Michael Gottfredson, eds. *Positive Criminology*. Beverly Hills, CA: Sage, 1987.

Johnson, Ray. *Ray Johnson's Total Security*. New York: NAL, 1984.

Kyte, Kathy. *Play It Safe: The Kid's Guide to Personal Safety and Crime Prevention*. New York: Knopf, 1983.

Levy, Barrie. *Dating Violence*. Seattle, WA: Seal Press, 1986.

Lipman, Ira. *How to Protect Yourself from Crime*, 3rd. ed. Chicago: Contemporary Books, 1989.

Long, Lynette, and Thomas Long. *The Handbook for Latchkey Children and Their Parents*. New York: Arbor, 1983.

Main, Ronald, and Jody Zervas. *Keep Your Kids Straight*. Blue Ridge Summit, PA: Tab, 1991.

McNamara, Joseph D. *Safe and Sane: The Sensible Way to Protect Yourself, Your Loved Ones, Your Property and Possessions*. New York: Perigee, 1984.

Myers, David G. *Social Psychology*, 3rd ed. New York: McGraw-Hill, 1990.

NiCarthy, Ginny. *Getting Free; A Handbook for Women in Abusive Relationships*. Seattle, WA: Seal Press, 1986.

Niehaus, Joseph. *The Sixth Sense: Practical Tips for Everyday Safety*. Tempe, AZ: Blue Bird, 1990.

Remley, Anne. "From Obedience to Independence." *Psychology Today* (October 1988): 56–59.

Rubington, Earl, and Martin Weinberg. *Deviance: The Interactionist Approach*, 5th ed. New York: Macmillan, 1987.

Sanday, Peggy R. "The Socio-Cultural Context of Rape." *Journal of Social Issues* 37 (1981): 5–27.

U.S. Department of Justice. *Sourcebook of Criminal Justice Statistics*. Washington, D.C.: U.S. Government Printing Office (issued annually).

Warshaw, Robin. *I Never Called It Rape*. New York: Harper, 1988.

Wattleton, Faye, and Elisabeth Keifer. *How to Talk with Your Child About Sexuality*. Garden City, NY: Doubleday, 1988.

Wells, Joel. *How to Survive with Your Teenager*. Chicago: Thomas More, 1982.

Whittemore, Gerald. *Street Wisdom for Women*. Boston: Quinlan, 1986.

Wright, James D. "Second Thoughts About Gun Control." *The Public Interest*, no. 91 (Spring 1988): 23–39.

York, Phyllis, David York, and Ted Wachtel. *Toughlove.* Garden City, NY: Doubleday, 1982.

For background information, the authors have drawn upon the continuing coverage of crime stories and crime issues in the *Los Angeles Times* and the *St. Louis Post-Dispatch*.